Cambridge Elements

Elements in Religion a
edited b
Paul K. Mc
Loyola University Chicago
Chad Meister
Bethel University

MONOTHEISM AND FAITH IN GOD

Ian G. Wallis

CAMBRIDGE
UNIVERSITY PRESS

CAMBRIDGE
UNIVERSITY PRESS

University Printing House, Cambridge CB2 8BS, United Kingdom

One Liberty Plaza, 20th Floor, New York, NY 10006, USA

477 Williamstown Road, Port Melbourne, VIC 3207, Australia

314–321, 3rd Floor, Plot 3, Splendor Forum, Jasola District Centre,
New Delhi – 110025, India

79 Anson Road, #06–04/06, Singapore 079906

Cambridge University Press is part of the University of Cambridge.

It furthers the University's mission by disseminating knowledge in the pursuit of
education, learning, and research at the highest international levels of excellence.

www.cambridge.org
Information on this title: www.cambridge.org/9781108970440
DOI: 10.1017/9781108980708

First published 2020

A catalogue record for this publication is available from the British Library.

ISBN 978-1-108-97044-0 Paperback
ISSN 2631-3014 (online)
ISSN 2631-3006 (print)

Cambridge University Press has no responsibility for the persistence or accuracy of
URLs for external or third-party internet websites referred to in this publication
and does not guarantee that any content on such websites is, or will remain,
accurate or appropriate.

Monotheism and Faith in God

Elements in Religion and Monotheism

DOI: 10.1017/9781108980708
First published online: November 2020

Ian G. Wallis

Author for correspondence: Ian G. Wallis, ian.wallis@sero.co.uk

Abstract: After offering a brief overview of the role of faith within Judaism, Christianity and Islam, an interdisciplinary analysis of faith, belief, belief systems and the act of believing is undertaken. The debate over the nature of doctrine between George Lindbeck and Alister McGrath brings into focus four ways in which beliefs can be employed: expressive, interpretative, formative and referential/relational. An analysis of monotheistic belief ensues which demonstrates how it can function meaningfully in each of these modes, including the last, where insights from phenomenology and relational ontology, as well as philosophical theology, favour a participatory approach in which God is encountered not as an object of investigation, but as that transcendent Other whose worship is the fulfilment of human being. The study concludes by highlighting convergences between the nature of faith presented in the initial scriptural overview and that developed throughout the rest of the study.

Keywords: faith, monotheism, being-in-relation, self-transcendence, participation

ISBNs: 9781108970440 (PB), 9781108980708 (OC)
ISSNs: 2631-3014 (online), 2631-3006 (print)

Contents

1 Faith in Judaism, Christianity and Islam

1.1 Setting the Scene

Before embarking on an exploration of the relationship between monotheism and faith, we should start by stating the obvious, namely that the nature of the latter (as, indeed, the former) is complex and nuanced. For example, there are both propositional (*fides quae creditor*; cf. orthodoxy) and dispositional (*fides qua creditur*; cf. orthopraxy) dimensions to faith, with much debate over how they relate to one another. Can you believe in a God of love whilst practising hatred or embody faith, hope and love whilst remaining an avowed atheist? Then there is the highly contentious question about the significance of faith within the salvific processes of a religion. Is faith a means of securing salvation and, if so, how does that sit within a system of belief rooted in divine grace? And does faith's salvific potential depend on believing aright or acting accordingly? Nor should we overlook the range of human aptitudes or responses constituting faith in its various manifestations: affirmation, allegiance, assent, assurance, belief, confidence, credibility, doctrine, endurance, faithfulness, fecundity, fidelity, integrity, knowledge, obedience, perception, perseverance, pledge, profession, security, steadfastness, testimony and trust, to name but a few.

All this begs the question of how faith can be identified and, indeed, whether it lends itself to precise or even meaningful definition. One approach is to focus on lexical stock (e.g. belief/faith in English, *credo/fides* in Latin, *pisteuô/pistis* in Greek, *âman* root in Hebrew, *îmân* root in Arabic, etc.), but the semantics of designated words are rarely, if ever, coterminous with the phenomenon they can denote.[1] So, for instance, whilst the righteous will live by 'faith/faithfulness' (*'emûnâh*, Habakkuk 2:4), Moses' hands were 'steady' (*'emûnâh*) until the sun set (Exodus 17:12) – the same Hebrew word is employed, but with very different meanings. Further, sometimes faith is assumed even when it is not specifically identified. Take Abraham's readiness to sacrifice his son, Isaac. The Genesis 22 account makes no mention of the patriarch's faith, although later Jewish, together with Christian and Islamic, interpretations make explicit what is surely implicit within the earliest version (e.g. Jubilees 17:15–18; 2 Maccabees 2:52; 4 Maccabees 16:19–22; Hebrews 11:17; Quran 37:111).

In the light of these observations, throughout the following survey of ancient Scriptures and their interpretative traditions, a nuanced approach has been adopted in which vocabulary associated with faith supplies a point of departure, whilst recognizing that even here context must determine whether particular

---

[1] James Barr, *The Semantics of Biblical Language* (Oxford: Oxford University Press, 1961), 161–205.

instantiations should be interpreted in this way. In turn, passages making explicit reference to faith with its attendant characteristics will alert us to its presence in other contexts where it is assumed or can be deduced. By proceeding in this manner, hopefully we will be able to supply an adequate account of the phenomenon under review without becoming so broad or ill-defined as to render the whole enterprise vacuous.

1.2 Sacred Belief in the Ancient World

Although, as we shall demonstrate shortly, faith-language features significantly within the scriptural traditions of the three principal monotheistic religions, they have no exclusive claim to it in the ancient world, where it finds expression in religious contexts with respect to both credulity over the existence of divine beings as well as their alleged oracles or wonders, and trust-like responses to the same.[2] With respect to the former, consider the following selection drawn from across the genres of ancient Greek literature:

> At any rate, one should not disbelieve the god (*tô theô goun ouk apistein eikos*) (Euripides [480–406 BCE], *Ion* 557 [LCL 10]). [F]or he [Aristodicus son of Heraclides] disbelieved the oracle and thought that those who had inquired of the god spoke untruly (*apisteôn te tô chrêsmô*) (Herodotus [c. 484–c. 425 BCE], *Histories* 1.158 [LCL 117]). Are we assured, then, that there are two causes, amongst those we previously discussed, which lead to faith in the gods (*tô . . . theôn . . . pistin*)? (Plato [c. 420–c. 348 BCE], *Laws* 12.966d [LCL 192]). Obviously then, he would not have given the counsel if he had not believed (*episteuen*) that what he said would come true. And who could have inspired him with such belief (*pisteuseien*) but a god (*theô*)? And since he had belief in the gods, how can he have questioned their existence (*pisteuôn de theois pôs ouk einai theous enomizen*)? (Xenophon [431–354 BCE], Memorabilia 1.1.5 [LCL 168*]).

Although less common, there are ancient texts where faith extends beyond credulity to embrace trust and fidelity. It is in this vein that the Athenian statesman Aristides (530–468 BCE) comments on the piety (*eusebeias*) of fellow civilians resulting from their faith in the gods (*dia tên pistin hên en tois theois eichon*; *Panathenaic Oration* 155 [LCL 533]). Or, again, Aristotle's (384–322 BCE) observation that 'Fortunate men stand in a certain relation to the divinity and love the gods (*to theion*), believing on the basis of the benefits they have received from fortune' (*pisteuontes dia ta gignomena agatha apo tês tychês*; *Rhetoric* 2.17 [LCL 193*]). No ancient author, however, engages in the spectrum of meanings and applications of faith in relation to the divine more

---

[2] For a fuller review, see Teresa Morgan, *Roman Faith and Christian Faith:* Pistis *and* Fides *in the Early Roman Empire and Early Churches* (Oxford: Oxford University Press, 2015), 122–75.

than the Greek biographer and essayist Plutarch (c. 50–c. 120 CE). As the following extended quotation illustrates, he recognized how belief in the gods could restrain destructive behaviour whilst supplying meaning and form to life, thereby engendering joy, hope and well-being:

> Now we should, I grant you, remove superstition (*deisidaimonian*) from our belief in the gods (*tês peri theôn doxês*) like a rheum from the eye; but if this proves impossible, we should not cut away both together and kill the faith that most men have in the gods (*tên pistin hên hoi pleistoi peri theôn echousin*) . . .. No, among mankind a few are afraid of God who would not be better off without that fear; for since they fear him as a ruler mild to the good and hating the wicked, by this one fear, which keeps them from doing wrong . . .. On the other hand the attitude toward God that we find in the ignorant but not greatly wicked majority of mankind contains no doubt along with the sense of reverence and honour an element of tremulous fear (and from this we get our term for superstition); but outweighing this a thousand times is the element of cheerful hope, of exultant joy, and whether in prayer or in thanksgiving of ascribing every furtherance of felicity to the gods. This is proved by the strongest kind of evidence: no visit delights us more than a visit to a temple; no occasion than a holy day; no act or spectacle than what we see and what we do ourselves in matters that involve the gods, whether we celebrate a ritual or take part in a choral dance or attend a sacrifice or ceremony of initiation. (*Moralia* 1101c [LCL 428])

One observation arising from this brief survey is that the language of belief can be employed in relation to divine beings and their alleged communications with mortals in a manner that implies no exclusive allegiance to a single deity. That is to say, whilst faith was increasingly being recognized as the currency of human–divine encounter, there was nothing inherently monotheistic about it. As the Graeco-Roman pantheons bear witness, it was quite possible not only to believe in the existence of multiple deities, but also to worship at their sanctuaries without any sense of compromise or infidelity.

That said, we should also note that philosophical monotheism has an ancient pedigree which reaches back through Aristotle's 'unmoved mover' (*proton akinêton*) and Plato's self-generating creative 'Demiurge' (*dêmiourgos*), both of whom are postulated through the application of deductive reasoning,[3] to the Greek polymath Xenophanes (570–475 BCE) who advocated, 'One god, the greatest among gods and men, neither in form like unto mortals nor in thought. He sees all over, thinks all over, and hears all over. But without toil he swayeth

---

[3] Aristotle discusses his 'unmoved mover' in *Physics* and *Metaphysics*, whilst Plato makes his case for a 'Demiurge' in *Timaeus*.

all things by the thought of his mind'.[4] Although the existence of other deities is not denied, we can discern here the beginning of a line of thinking which Aristotle works through to its logical conclusion. Interestingly, Aristotle could use the language of belief in relation to his monotheistic contentions: 'So from these considerations one would be led to believe (*pisteuseien*) that there is a prime mover (*proton akinêton*), itself unmoved; and the conviction is strengthened by a consideration of the initiating principles of the (more familiar) agents of motion' (*Physics* 259a [LCL 255]).

1.3 Faith in Judaism

On turning to Judaism, few figures come into focus as paradigms of faith with greater clarity than Abraham (Abram).[5] The earliest sources of the Pentateuch, the Yahwist ('J', 950–850 BCE) and the Elohist ('E', 850–750 BCE), present the patriarch as a gratuitous recipient of divine favour in the form of land to inherit and an heir to inhabit it, through which his burgeoning people would become a source of blessing to all nations. According to Genesis 12 (J), Abraham and Sarah (Sarai), despite their advancing years, respond obediently and set off from their homeland. In chapter 15, however, which may well be another version of the same foundational memory or event (E?), Abraham questions how this can come about given his wife is beyond the age of fertility. Subsequent divine reassurance elicits what becomes a definitive response: 'And he believed (*he'e-min*) the LORD; and the LORD reckoned it to him as righteousness' (15:6).[6] Although both 'reckon' (*khâshab*) and 'righteousness' (*tsedâkah*) can carry forensic connotations, the context does not favour such a meaning, although later interpretations would reach a different conclusion.[7] Instead, a relational

---

[4] *Fragments* 23–5 (John Burnet, *Early Greek Philosophy*, 3rd ed. [London: A. & C. Black, 1920], chapter 2, §57).

[5] The literature on Abraham is vast – here is a selection. Primary sources: Louis Ginzberg, *The Legends of the Jews*, trans. Henrietta Szold and Paul Radin, 5 vols. (Philadelphia: Jewish Publication Society of America, 1909–38) and James L. Kugel, *The Bible as It Was* (Cambridge, MA: Harvard University Press, 1997), 131–48. Historicity: John van Seters, *Abraham in History and Tradition* (New Haven, CT: Yale University Press, 1975) and Thomas L. Thompson, *The Historicity of the Patriarchal Narratives: The Quest for the Historical Abraham* (Berlin: Walter de Gruyter, 1974). Ecumenical approaches: Karl-Josef Kuschel, *Abraham: A Symbol of Hope for Jews, Christians and Muslims*, trans. John Bowden (London: SCM, 1995) and Jon D. Levenson, *Inheriting Abraham: The Legacy of the Patriarch in Judaism, Christianity and Islam* (Princeton: Princeton University Press, 2014).

[6] Unless indicated to the contrary, all biblical translations come from the *New Revised Standard Version*.

[7] For example, 'And he had faith in the word of the Lord and it was reckoned to him for merit because he did not argue before him with words' (Targum Pseudo-Jonathan on Genesis 15:6 [trans. John Bowker, *The Targums and Rabbinic Literature: An Introduction to Jewish Interpretations of Scripture* (Cambridge: Cambridge University Press, 1969), 201]); 'That God marvelling at Abraham's faith in Him repaid him with faithfulness by confirming with an oath the

dynamic seems more apt where faith becomes the medium for 'right-relating' with God. Equally, the context stresses the trusting complexion of faith, albeit a trust precipitating concrete action: there would be no offspring without conjugal relations and no land without adventure. Inherent, then, to faith is risk and vulnerability, as the familiar world of past experience gives way to liminality where the contours are drawn by divine promise and its ensuing possibilities.

Interestingly, later interpreters of Abraham's faith place the stress upon his faithfulness or obedience, either in general terms (e.g. Nehemiah 9:7–8; Jubilees 17:15–18; 2 Maccabees 1:2) or with specific reference to his willingness to sacrifice Isaac, the sole heir of God's promises (Genesis 22:1–19) – the incident which above all becomes emblematic of the patriarch's *'emûnâh*:

> And the LORD called Abraham by his name again from heaven just as he caused us to appear so that we might speak to him in the name of the LORD. And he said, 'I swear by myself, says the LORD, because you have done this thing and you have not denied your firstborn son, whom you love, to me that I shall surely bless you and I shall surely multiply your seed like the stars of heaven and like the sand of the seashore and your seed will inherit the cities of their enemies. And all of the nations of the earth will bless themselves by your seed because you obeyed my word. And I have made known to all that you are faithful to me in everything which I say to you. Go in peace'. (Jubilees 18:14–16 [*OTP*]; also Sirach 44:19–21; 2 Maccabees 2:52; 4 Maccabees 16:19–25)

Perhaps unsurprisingly, given its importance within an emerging Israelite/Jewish identity, Abraham's paradigmatic role extends to embrace Torah observance. As early as the second century BCE, he is portrayed as the one who 'kept the law of the Most High, and entered into a covenant with him; he certified the covenant in his flesh, and when he was tested he proved faithful' (Sirach 44:20; also Jubilees 6:17–19). The Alexandrian Jew, Philo (20 BCE–50 CE), aware of the anachronistic nature of such a claim, explains how it was possible given the Torah had not been communicated to Moses, taking his cue from a verse in Genesis (26:5): 'He [Abraham] did them, not taught by written words, but unwritten nature gave him the zeal to follow where wholesome and untainted impulse led him. And when they have God's promises before them what should men do but trust in them most firmly?' (*peri de hôn ho theos homologei, ti prosêken anthrôpous ê bebaiotata pisteuein*) (*On Abraham* 275; 'one who obeyed the law', 276 [LCL 289]; also Mishnah, Kiddushin 4.14).

This passage from Philo alerts us to the continuing appreciation of the trust-like qualities of faith, in addition to the emphasis on faithful

---

gifts which He had promised, and here He no longer talked with him as God with man but as a friend with a familiar' (Philo, *On Abraham* 273 [LCL 289]).

obedience. Further, such trusting belief is celebrated in the Babylonian Talmud where Jews are described as 'believers and descendants of believers' (Shabbat 97a) and even gains meritorious significance in rabbinic theology where Abraham is cited as an exemplar once again:

> Shema'yah says: 'The faith with which their father Abraham believed in Me is deserving that I should divide the sea for them'. For it is said: 'And he believed in the Lord' (Gen 15:6). Abtalyon says: 'The faith with which they believed in Me is deserving that I should divide the sea for them'. For it is said: 'And the people believed' (Ex 4:31) . . . . And so also you find that our father Abraham inherited both this world and the world beyond only as a reward for the faith with which he believed, as it is said: 'And he believed in the Lord', etc. (Gen 15:6). (Mekilta de Rabbi Ishmael on Exodus 14:15 and 14:31 [trans. J. Z. Lauterbach (Philadelphia: Jewish Publication Society of America, 1933)])

Retrospectively, Abraham serves not only as the archetypal Torah observer, but also monotheist. Notably, his exclusive allegiance to Yahweh, Israel's God, although implied, is not made explicit in the earliest Pentateuchal sources. Later traditions associate Abraham's departure from Haran and, by implication, the deities of his homeland in quest of the promised land as a movement from idolatry or polytheism to belief in one true God. This framing of the patriarch as a monotheist appears to be linked with the broader monotheizing reforms of the sixth century BCE reflected in the Deuteronomistic history (e.g. Joshua 24:2–4) which, judging from the book of Jubilees, was well established by the second century BCE (e.g. 11:14–17; 12:1–14). Further evidence of this growing commitment to monotheism is supplied by another re-telling of Israelite history, *Pseudo-Philo* or *Biblical Antiquities* (first century CE): 'And when all those inhabiting the land were being led astray after their own devices, Abraham believed in me and was not led astray with them. And I rescued him from the flame *and took* him *and brought him over all the land of Canaan* and said to him in a vision, *"To your seed I will give this land"'* (23.5 [*OTP*]). What is not so clear from these texts is whether they bear witness to an exclusive allegiance to one God, without denying the existence of other deities (e.g. monolatry or henotheism), or a thoroughgoing monotheism which excludes this possibility. On turning to Josephus and Philo, however, we find the latter position espoused:

> He [Abraham] was thus the first boldly to declare that God, the creator of the universe, is one, and that, if any other being contributed aught to man's welfare, each did so by His command and not in virtue of its own inherent power. (Josephus, *Jewish Antiquities* 1.154–7 [LCL 242])
>
> In this creed [pantheism] Abraham had been reared, and for a long time remained a Chaldean. Then opening the soul's eye as though after profound sleep, and beginning to see the pure beam instead of the deep darkness, he

followed the ray and discerned what he had not beheld before, a charioteer and pilot presiding over the world and directing in safety his own work, assuming the charge and superintendence of that work and of all such parts of it as are worthy of the divine care. (Philo, *On Abraham* 70 [LCL 289])

Whether the Jewish Scriptures, when viewed diachronically, disclose an evolutionary process in which monotheistic Yahwism emerges from the polytheism of Canaanite religion or whether that same literature evidences a monotheizing tendency from the outset remains a matter of debate.[8] What can be claimed with confidence is that Israelite identity increasingly becomes grounded in the conviction that Yahweh is the sole creator and sovereign of the universe who has elected and entered into covenant with a chosen people who, in response, are bound to offer their exclusive allegiance and devotion. Such a conviction is reflected, for example, in the daily recitation of the Shema[9] and the lengthy prayer known as the Eighteen Benedictions.[10] However, it is quite possible that the Nash Papyrus, dated to the second century BCE and containing the Hebrew text of the Decalogue and Shema, suggests that this practice has a considerably longer pedigree. Through exposure to different philosophical systems and religious traditions, Jewish belief in monotheism becomes absolute and is ascribed creedal status as adumbrated in the Thirteen Principles of Maimonides (1135–1204 CE): 'I believe with perfect faith (*'ani m'amin be'emunâh shelêmâh*) that the Creator, Blessed be His Name, is the Creator and Guide of everything that has been created; He alone has made, does make, and will make all things. I believe with perfect faith that the Creator, Blessed be His Name, is One, and that there is no unity in any manner like His, and that He alone is our God, who was, and is, and will be'.[11]

Before drawing our review of faith in early Judaism to a close, it should be noted that Israelite religion was probably not the earliest incidence of

---

[8] See Richard Bauckham, 'Biblical Theology and the Problems of Monotheism', in Craig Bartholomew et al. (eds.), *Out of Egypt: Biblical Theology and Biblical Interpretation* (Milton Keynes: Paternoster, 2004), 187–232.

[9] 'Hear, O Israel: The LORD is our God, the LORD alone. You shall love the LORD your God with all your heart, and with all your soul, and with all your might' (Deuteronomy 6:4–5). The rabbinic form included three scriptural passages (Deuteronomy 6:4–9; 11:13–21; Numbers 15:37–41) plus additional blessings. The twice-daily recitation is prescribed in the Mishnah (Berakoth 1.1–4) and may reflect a post-70 CE practice, although Jesus appears to have been familiar with Shema recitation (cf. Mark 12:28–34).

[10] 'You are praised, O Lord our God and God of our fathers ... God Supreme, Creator of heaven and earth ... Holy are You, and awe-inspiring is Your Name; and beside You there is no God' (1, 3 [trans. Jakob Petuchowski, *The Lord's Prayer and Jewish Liturgy* (London: Burns & Oates, 1978), 27–30]). Also known as the *Tefillah* or *Shemoneh Esreh*, the Eighteen Benedictions probably reached its final form in response to the rise of Christianity (cf. twelfth petition). As with the Shema, the Mishnah prescribes, in this case, thrice-daily recitation (Berakoth 4.1).

[11] Principles 1–2; trans. *The Authorised Daily Prayer Book of the United Hebrew Congregation of the Commonwealth* (Cambridge: Cambridge University Press, 1992), 154.

a monotheizing tendency. For instance, significantly earlier, a young Egyptian pharaoh, Amenophis IV (c. 1385 BCE), earned a reputation for demanding exclusive allegiance to the sun deity Aten to the extent that he eventually changed his name to Akhenaten. Whether his reforms reflect a thoroughgoing rejection of all permutations of polytheism remains a matter of debate, although some of the texts associated with him appear to point in that direction. For instance, the following excerpts from the Great Hymn to Aten are inscribed within the tomb of Ay, Tutankhamun's successor, in Amarna, a city built by Akhenaten:

> O sole God who has no equal,
> thou didst create the earth after thy heart, thou alone,
> with people, cattle and all kind of game,
> all on earth that walk on legs,
> all in the sky that fly on wings,
>
> Foreign countries, Canaan and Nubia,
> thou settest every man in his place,
> and createst what they need.
> Everybody has his food,
> his lifetime has been fixed ...
>
> Thou createst millions of forms from thyself, the One:
> cities and villages, fields, road and river ...
>
> Thou art the one who created when nothing was there,
> who created everything as it came forth from thy mouth.[12]

1.4 Faith in Christianity

During the first century CE, when Jewishness was increasingly becoming an ethnic identity inherited through birth, the Jesus movement was extending beyond that matrix to embrace non-Jews. Initially, this expansion precipitated a crisis over Christian identity which is addressed in a number of New Testament books, notably Acts, Romans and Galatians, whilst implied in others (e.g. Matthew, John, Hebrews). The apostle Paul, in particular, champions faith as the defining characteristic and appeals to Abraham for precedent and

---

[12] Trans. Johannes C. de Moor, *The Rise of Yahwism: The Roots of Israelite Monotheism* (Leuven: Leuven University Press, 1990), 43. De Moor discusses the monotheistic credentials of Atenism, as does James K. Hoffmeier, *Akhenaten and the Origins of Monotheism* (Oxford: Oxford University Press, 2015). On the origins of monotheism within Israelite religion, see Mark S. Smith, *The Origins of Biblical Monotheism: Israel's Polytheistic Background and the Ugaritic Texts* (Oxford: Oxford University Press, 2001).

scriptural authority.[13] In Romans 4, it is the patriarch's trusting faith, rather than Jewish identity markers such as circumcision and Torah observance, that forms the basis for his right-relating to God and, as such, he embodies the archetypal human response to divine grace: 'The purpose was to make him the ancestor of all who believe (*pantôn tôn pisteuontôn*) without being circumcised and who thus have righteousness reckoned to them, and likewise the ancestor of the circumcised who are not only circumcised but who also follow the example of the faith (*tês ... pisteôs*) that our ancestor Abraham had before he was circumcised' (4:11–12). Paul develops a similar line of argument in Galatians 3 where he also, in what some scholars consider to be an exegetical sleight of hand, stresses how in Genesis 17, Yahweh's covenant was forged with Abraham and his seed in the singular (*sperma*), clearly a collective noun, before presenting Jesus Christ as that seed and means by which God would bring everyone into right relationship through faith:

> Now the promises were made to Abraham and to his offspring; it does not say, 'And to offsprings', as of many; but it says, 'And to your offspring', that is, to one person, who is Christ .... Therefore the law was our disciplinarian until Christ came, so that we might be justified by faith (*ek pisteôs*). But now that faith (*tês pisteôs*) has come, we are no longer subject to a disciplinarian [i.e. the law], for in Christ Jesus you are all children of God through faith (*tês pisteôs*). (3:16, 24–6)

As noted with respect to Judaism, the nature of faith is also explored in relation to Abraham in early Christianity. The previous paragraph emphasizes the trusting quality of faith, whereas the epistle of James stresses its behavioural expression which becomes a measure of faith's veracity:

> Was not our ancestor Abraham justified by works when he offered his son Isaac on the altar? You see that faith (*hê pistis*) was active along with his works, and faith (*hê pistis*) was brought to completion by the works. Thus the scripture was fulfilled that says, 'Abraham believed God (*episteusen ... tô theô*), and it was reckoned to him as righteousness', and he was called the friend of God. You see that a person is justified by works and not by faith alone (*ek pisteôs monon*) .... For just as the body without the spirit is dead, so faith without works is also dead (*hê pistis chôris ergôn nekra estin*). (James 2:21–4, 26)

---

[13] See Morgan, *Roman Faith*, 212–305. But note also the Fourth Gospel where faith as recognition and profession of Jesus' theological significance are stressed (e.g. 3:16–18; 6:35; 11:25–27) and where Jesus performs signs to engender it (e.g. 2:11; 11:47–48; 20:30–31). Authentic belief must perceive and affirm the true significance of these portents (cf. 12:37–40), to the extent that it is able to remain steadfast when exposed to personal scrutiny, challenging teaching or threatening circumstances (cf. 6:60–71; 9:1–38; 21:15–19). Again, see Morgan, *Roman Faith*, 394–443.

We also find that the patriarch becomes the guarantor of the credal content of faith. For example, according to the church historian Eusebius (263–339 CE), Abraham is the archetypal monotheist: 'for it was by faith towards the Logos of God (*pistei . . . tou theou logon*), the Christ who had appeared to him, that he was justified, and gave up the superstition of his fathers, and his former erroneous life, and confessed the God who is over all to be one (*hena . . . ton . . . theon*)' (*Ecclesiastical History* 1.4 [LCL 153]).

Interestingly, this brings into focus the uniquely Christian understanding of monotheism, namely its capacity for embracing distinct characterization, without divisibility, within divine essence.[14] One of the passages regularly employed in early doctrinal development is Genesis 18, where Abraham and Sarah offer hospitality to three guests who appear as one. The phrase, 'Abraham saw three, but worshipped only one', usually attributed to Origen (184–253 CE), became a refrain in Christological formulation where, prefiguring the Incarnation, faith discerns the presence of Christ accompanied by a pair of supporting angels.[15] Increasingly, though, this passage supplies biblical precedent for the Trinity as evidenced by the Christian rhetorician, Procopius of Gaza (465–528 CE): 'Some take the three men as three angels; the Judaizers, however, say that one of the three is God, while the other two are angels; others still deem them to bear the type of the holy and consubstantial Trinity, who are addressed as "Lord" in the singular'.[16]

The Christian interpretation of this passage and imbuing of Abraham's faith with Christian beliefs emphasizes the importance of orthodoxy or right-believing within the emerging church. Whilst Constantine's decision to adopt Christianity as the official religion of the Roman Empire exerted considerable pressure upon bishops to agree on an official version, the importance of right-believing emerged much earlier and is evidenced in a number of New Testament books. For example, Paul defends his version of the Gospel against those promulgated by Judaizing Christian missionaries at Galatia (Galatians 1:6–9; 3:1–14; 5:2–15), whilst challenging factional behaviour on confessional grounds at Corinth (1 Corinthians 1.11–13). The author of the Pastoral Epistles places great emphasis upon 'sound teaching' and 'soundness of

---

[14] Bogdan G. Bucur draws attention to a partial parallel in Philo of Alexandria's interpretation of Genesis 18 where God is accompanied by two powers, creative and kingly (*On Abraham* 121–2); see his 'The Early Christian Reception of Genesis 18: From Theophany to Trinitarian Symbolism', *Journal of Early Christian Studies* 23 (2015), 247.

[15] E.g. Hilary of Poitiers (310–368 CE), *On the Trinity* 4.25, 27.

[16] *Commentary of Genesis* 18 [Bucur]; however, Bucur also picks up an earlier trinitarian application in Augustine (354–430 CE), 'Early Christian Reception', 256–7.

faith'.[17] It would seem, then, that the dangers posed by false teachers and prophets, as well as of committing apostasy, emerged from the outset[18] and, partially in response, brief credal formulations started to appear:

> ... if you confess with your lips that Jesus is Lord and believe in your heart that God raised him from the dead (Romans 10:9) ... yet for us there is one God, the Father, from whom are all things and for whom we exist, and one Lord, Jesus Christ, through whom are all things and through whom we exist (1 Corinthians 8:6) ... Jesus is Lord (1 Corinthians 12:3) ..... There is one body and one Spirit, just as you were called to the one hope of your calling, one Lord, one faith, one baptism, one God and Father of all, who is above all and through all and in all (Ephesians 4:4–6) .. ... For there is one God; there is also one mediator between God and humankind, Christ Jesus, himself human, who gave himself a ransom for all – this was attested at the right time. (1 Timothy 2:5–6; also 1 Corinthians 15:3–5; Philippians 2:6–11; 1 Timothy 3:16; 6:13–14)

These, in turn, gave way to fuller 'rules of faith' (*kanôn tês pisteôs, regula fidei*), sometimes referred to as 'rules of truth' (*kanôn tês alêtheias, regula veritatis*), in the second and third centuries, such as the following from the writings of the influential African theologian, Tertullian (160–225 CE):

> The Rule of Faith, indeed, is altogether one, alone immovable and irreformable, the rule, to wit, of believing in one and only God omnipotent, Creator of the universe, and his Son Jesus Christ, born of the virgin Mary, crucified under Pontius Pilate, raised again the third day from the dead, received in the heavens, sitting now at right of the Father, destined to come to judge the quick and the dead through resurrection of the flesh as well [as of the Spirit].[19]

Such distillations of essential belief, often transmitted orally and only revealed to catechumens at baptism, not only supplied a credal framework for Christian identity, but also acted as a doctrinal filter for determining which books should constitute Scripture and then served as a hermeneutical key for interpreting the same.[20] By the fourth century and possibly earlier, these *regula* had evolved into the great ecumenical creeds and shaped the canon of Scripture – the foundations of orthodoxy – illustrating this insightful assessment of Christianity:

---

[17] 'Sound teaching': *hygiainousê didaskalia/logos* – 1 Timothy 1:10; 6:3; 2 Timothy 1:13; 4:3; Titus 2:1; also 1 Timothy 4:6; 'soundness of faith': *hygiainousê pistis* – Titus 1:13; 2:2.

[18] E.g. Matthew 7:15–23; Mark 13:22; Hebrews 6:1–12; 2 Peter 2:1–22; 1 John 2:18–28; 4:1–6; Revelation 2–3.

[19] *Veiling of Virgins* 1 (*ANCL* 4). Important *regula* can also be found in the writings of Irenaeus (b. 130 CE), Origen (184–253 CE), and Novatian (200–258 CE), amongst others, as well as in the early church orders of Hippolytus and the *Didascalia Apostolorum*. Richard Hanson offers a detailed analysis in *Tradition in the Early Church* (London: SCM, 1962), 75–129.

[20] On the role of 'rules of faith' in the early church, see also Lee Martin McDonald, *The Biblical Canon: Its Origin, Transmission, and Authority* (Ada, MI: Baker Academic, 2006), 38–69.

Christianity is the only major religion to set such store by creeds and doctrines. Other religions have scriptures, others have their characteristic ways of worship, others have their own peculiar ethics and lifestyle; other religions also have philosophical, intellectual or mystical forms as well as more popular manifestations. But except in response to Christianity, they have not developed creeds, statements of standard belief to which the orthodox are supposed to adhere. Other religions have hymns and prayers, they have festivals, they have popular myths, stories of saints and heroes, they have art forms, and have moulded whole societies and cultures. But they have no orthodoxy, a sense of right belief which is doctrinally sound and from which deviation means heresy.[21]

1.5 Faith in Islam

'O you who believe!' (*yâayyuhâ alladhîna âmanû!*) is probably the most attested exhortation in the entire Quran. In fact, of the three scriptural canons of the monotheistic religions, the language of faith (*îmân*) is most prevalent in the Quran, whether in relation to the believer (*mu'min*) or the infidel (*kâfir*), who may or may not be a Muslim, or the heretic (*takfir*). Foundational to the Muslim conception of faith is the oneness of God, which is affirmed repeatedly in Scripture[22] and encapsulated in the first clause of the principal Islamic profession, *Shahâdah*: 'There is no god, but God/Allah' (*lâ ilâha illa'Llâh*).[23]

Interestingly, the figure celebrated as the archetypal monotheist and, therefore, Muslim is none other than Abraham (*Ib'râhîm*): 'Abraham was neither Jew nor Christian, but rather was a ḥanîf, a submitter (*mus'liman*), and he was

---

[21] Frances Young, *The Making of the Creeds* (London: SCM, 1991), 1. At least from the fifth century, the Apostles' Creed was thought to have been composed by Jesus' first disciples – a view challenged from the fifteenth century and now largely rejected. Our earliest witness comes from the eighth century, although it probably has its roots in the Old Roman Creed, attested from the fourth century – roughly, coterminus with the Nicene Creed (325 CE) which, following the Arian controversy, became the Nicene-Constantinopolitan Creed (381 CE).

[22] E.g. Quran 2:163, 255; 3:2, 6, 18, 62; 6:102, 106; 7:158; 9:31; 16:2; 20:8, 14, 98; 23:116; 27:26; 28:70, 88; 35:3; 39:6; 40:3, 62, 65; 44:8; 59:22–23; 64:13; 73:9. Unless otherwise stated, we have used the following English translation of the Quran: *The Study Quran: A New Translation and Commentary*, edited by Seyyed Hossein Nasr et al (New York: HarperOne, 2015). Transliterations of the Arabic have been taken from: *The Noble Qur'an: A Word for Word Interlinear Translation Based on the Qur'an Arabic Corpus*, by Kais Dukes (Al Sadiqin, 2011).

[23] Quran 37:35; 47:19; also 2:163, 255. Although the two clauses of the full *Shahâdah*, 'There is no god, but God/Allah. Muhammad is the Messenger of God/Allah', are attested separately in the Quran (cf. 48:29), they are not found together and only begin to emerge as a formula towards the late seventh century CE where they appear in different variations on Islamic coins and building inscriptions, including the Dome of the Rock in Jerusalem. Whilst the *Shahâdah* is authoritative across the major interpretative trajectories of Islam, Shias add the phrase, 'Ali is the friend of God', in recognition of the elevated status of Muhammad's cousin and son-in-law, Ali ibn Abi Talib (c. 597–661 CE), as their first Imam. For further background, see the article on *Shahâdah* in *Encyclopedia of Islam*, edited by Juan E. Campo (New York: Facts on File, 2009), 618–19.

not one of the idolaters. Truly the people worthiest of Abraham are those who followed him, and this prophet and those who believe (*âmanû*). And God is the Protector of the believers (*l-mu'minîna*)' (3:67–8). 'He was not one of the idolaters' is something of a refrain for Abraham in the Quran and helps to reinforce his monotheistic credentials,[24] which are sometimes contrasted with those of Jews and Christians whose monotheism is compromised by, for example, Trinitarian proclivities[25] or a failure to embrace the 'creed of Abraham' (*millati Ib'râhîma*).[26] The word translated here as 'creed', *millah*, can also mean 'community', 'law' or 'way' and, although the meaning of this phrase is never defined in the Quran, it would appear to be coterminous with embracing the Islamic path of submission to the one God, recognition of his prophet, Muhammad,[27] and participation in the community (*ummah*) consti-tuted by these commitments, as can be inferred from the following excerpt:

> And [remember] when his Lord tried Abraham with [certain] words, and he fulfilled them. He said, 'I am making you an imam for mankind'. He said, 'And of my progeny?' He said, 'My covenant does not include the wrongdoers' .. ... 'And, our Lord, make us submit (*mus'limayni*) unto Thee, and from our progeny a community submitting (*mus'limatan*) unto Thee, and show us our rites, and relent unto us. Truly Thou art the Relenting, the Merciful. Our Lord, raise up in their midst a messenger from among them, who will recite Thy signs to them, and will teach them the Book and Wisdom, and purify them. Truly Thou art the Mighty, the Wise'. And who shuns the creed of Abraham (*millati ib'râhîma*), but a foolish soul? We chose him in the world and in the Hereafter he shall be among the righteous. And when his Lord said unto him, 'Submit (*aslim*)!' he said, 'I submit (*aslamtu*) to the Lord of the worlds'. And Abraham enjoined the same upon his children .. ... And they say, 'Be Jews or Christians and you shall be rightly guided'. Say, 'Rather, [ours is] the creed of Abraham (*millata ib'râhîma*), a *ḥanîf*, and he was not of the idolaters'. Say, 'We believe in God (*âmannâ bil-lahi*), and in that which was sent down unto us, and in that which was sent down unto Abraham, Ishmael, Isaac, Jacob, and the Tribes, and in what Moses and Jesus were given, and in what the prophets were given from their Lord. We make no distinction among any of them, and unto Him we submit (*mus'limûna*)'. And

---

[24] E.g. 3:67, 95; 6:79, 161; 16:120, 123; Abraham's monotheistic credentials: 2:130, 135; 3:95; 4:125; 12:38; 16:123; 22:78.

[25] 'O People of the Book! Do not exaggerate in your religion, nor utter anything concerning God save the truth. Verily the Messiah, Jesus son of Mary, was only a messenger of God, and His Word, which He committed to Mary, and a Spirit from Him. So believe in God and His messengers, and say not "Three". Refrain!' (4:171).

[26] E.g. 2:130, 135; 3:95; 4:125; 12:38; 16:123; 22:78.

[27] Cf. 'The Quran suggests that Muslims have an advantage over other monotheists in following the creed of Abraham, since the claim that Abraham was a Jew or a Christian is rejected (2:140; 3:65–7) and elsewhere Abraham and his creed are explicitly connected to the Prophet Muhammad and his religious community (2:135; 3:68; 6:61; 16:123)'. *The Study Quran*, 248.

if they believe (*âmanû*) in the like of what you believe (*âmantum*) in, then
they shall be rightly guided. And if they turn away, then they are merely in
schism and God will suffice you against them, and He is the Hearing, the
Knowing. (Quran 2:124, 128–32, 135–7)

These verses highlight a number of key issues that shaped different schools of
Islamic theology; first, the relation between *islâm* (submission) and *îmân*
(faith), where the former is either seen as embracing the latter or vice versa.[28]
For instance, according to the *Hadith of Gabriel*, a definitive summary of Islam
for Sunnis recorded in two authoritative collections:

Muhammad al-Bukhari (810–70 CE)

islâm – worship Allah alone, prayers, almsgiving, fasting (Ramadan).
îmân – believe in Allah, his angels, his messengers, the resurrection and
    meeting Allah.

Muslim ibn al-Hajjâj (817/18–874/5 CE)

islâm – profession (*shahâdah*), prayer, almsgiving, fasting (Ramadan),
    pilgrimage.
îmân – believe in Allah, his angels, his books, his messengers, day of judge-
    ment, predestination.

There are significant variations here, whilst demonstrating considerable consensus. Furthermore, both versions include a third component, *ihsân*, which is
usually translated as 'perfection' and refers to the offering of perfect worship as
if in the presence of Allah. Given what has already been included, however,
ihsân is often understood in terms of living out the way of life delineated by
islâm and *îmân* – that is to say, to embody them and so become an exemplary
Muslim.[29]

Second, these verses from Sura 2 (The Cow) stress the importance not simply
of a trusting faith, but of the substance of belief, where at least two dimensions
are brought into focus. Initially, the content of believing aright is stressed in
comparison with Jews and Christians, who, although viewed sympathetically,
ultimately prove to be in error for failing to embrace the creed of Abraham,
which, as we have suggested, extends beyond monotheistic belief to include
recognition of the significance of Muhammad and participation in the Muslim
way of life:

Truly those who disbelieve in God and His messengers, and seek to make
a distinction between God and His messengers, and say, 'We believe in some

---

[28] See the discussion of Toshihko Izutsu, *The Concept of Belief in Islamic Theology: A Semantic
Analysis of Imân and Islâm* (Lahore: Suhail Academy, 2005 [this edition]), esp. 57–82.

[29] Again, Izutsu, *Concept of Belief*, chapter 4.

and disbelieve in others', and seek to take a way between – it is they who are truly disbelievers, and We have prepared for the disbelievers a humiliating punishment. But those who believe in God and His messengers and make no distinction between any of them – unto them He will give their rewards. (Quran 4:150–2)

Although Jews and Christians are not explicitly mentioned here, the inference is clear. Later Islamic theological reflection explores whether a trusting faith in Allah constituted of itself a sufficient Islamic response or whether believing aright was necessary and, if so, whether right belief could only be derived through revelation or could only, or also, be deduced through reason. The contemporary Islamic scholar, Abdul Khaliq Kazi, offers the following summary:

> Khâriji: *Îmân* is belief in heart and profession of that belief through the tongue accompanied with abstinence from *all* sins. Mu'tazilah and Shîrî: *Îmân* is belief in heart and profession of that belief through tongue accompanied with abstinence from *major* sins. Shâfi'î and Ahl al-Hadîth: *Îmân* is word and deed; acts of obedience are part of *îmân*; but *îmân* is possible without corresponding deeds, i.e., man will not be declared an infidel without them. Mâturîdî: It is belief in heart and its profession by tongue. Ash'arî: It is belief in heart only. Murji'ah: It is knowledge of God only *plus* profession. Karrâmî: It is profession of the tongue only.[30]

Third, the second dimension concerning substance relates to the nature of belief in terms of response to the divine. Abraham's faith extended beyond intellectual assent – believing aright – to wholehearted commitment epitomized in submission. Here we touch on another rich seam of thought which explores, for example, whether fulfilment of *islâm* and *îmân* as prescribed in the *Hadith of Gabriel* defines Islam or whether *ihsân* is also essential and, if so, whether this entailed work (*'amal*).[31] This, in turn, raises questions revolving around whether belief could increase and decrease, especially with respect to righteous deeds performed or left undone and, by implication, to repentance.[32] In the light of these comments, it is evident that both orthodoxy and orthopraxy feature significantly, albeit in different measures and to varying degrees, in the

---

[30] Abdul Khaliq Kazi, 'The Meaning of *Îmân* and *Islâm* in the Qur'ân', *Islamic Studies* 5 (1966), 228, our underlining.

[31] Izutsu, *Concept of Belief*, chapter 9.

[32] 'Only they are believers whose hearts quake with fear when God is mentioned, and when His signs are recited unto them, they increase them in faith, and they trust in their Lord, who perform the prayer and spend from that which We have provided them. It is they who truly are believers' (8:2–4). 'Truly those who disbelieve after having believed, then increase in disbelief, their repentance shall not be accepted, and they are the ones who are astray' (3:90; also 3:173; 4:137).

interpretative trajectories that characterized Islam from the outset and continue to do so:

> But for those who believe and perform righteous deeds, We shall cause them to enter Gardens with rivers running below, abiding therein forever. God's Promise is true, and who is truer in speech than God? It will not be in accordance with your desires nor the desires of the People of the Book. Whosoever does evil shall be requited for it, and he will find no protector or helper for himself apart from God. And whosoever performs righteous deeds, whether male or female, and is a believer, such shall enter the Garden, and they shall not be wronged so much as the speck on a date stone. And who is better in religion than the one who submits his face to God, and is virtuous, and follows the creed of Abraham, as a *ḥanīf*? And God did take Abraham for a friend. (Quran 4:122–5)

1.6 Conclusion

Drawing this brief overview to a close, a number of observations can be made. First, faith as a response to the sacred predates Israelite religion, as does exclusive commitment to a single divine being. However, we noted that certain expressions of faith were not necessarily deemed incompatible with belief in the existence of multiple deities or even allegiance to the same. Moving on to our review of Judaism, Christianity and Islam, we noted that although faith emerges from different circumstances, is orientated around different convictions and finds expression in different forms, there is significant common ground. In particular, there is a wholehearted commitment to monotheism, albeit conceived differently, as well as a concern for the substance of belief, both in terms of its dispositional and propositional content and the relation between belief and conduct. Equally important to all three is the relation between faith and participation in a very particular species of community life conceived out of each religion's fundamental convictions and designed not only to inculcate faith in its participants, but also to engender a sense of shared inheritance, identity, vocation and destiny.[33]

2 Faith and Belief

2.1 An Important Distinction

Having offered a brief overview of the central role of faith within the three principal monotheistic religions, we turn attention to the anatomy of faith and belief per se. So far, these terms have been used interchangeably, but a number of scholars have sought to distinguish between them, at least to some measure. The

---

[33] On the community-creating capacity of faith, see especially Morgan, *Roman Faith*, esp. 473–500.

specialist in comparative religion, Wilfred Cantwell Smith, when exploring possible commonalities between religions, suggests 'faith is that quality of or available to humankind by which we are characterized as transcending, or are enabled to transcend, the natural order'.[34] Or, again, the American theologian specializing in human development, James Fowler, describes faith as 'an active mode of being and committing, a way of moving into and giving shape to our experiences of life ... faith is always relational ... faith is our way of discerning and committing ourselves to the centres of value and power that exert ordering force in our lives'.[35] Both Smith and Fowler have been accused of so generalizing faith as to place it beyond the reach of critical investigation. Furthermore, especially in the case of Smith, his claim that faith can be distilled from religions has been challenged.[36]

It is questionable, however, whether these criticisms are sustainable. Consider a partial analogy. Few would question that the desire to communicate, to relate to that which is beyond self, was a significant driver in the evolution of language; yet equally, language, once acquired, greatly enhances our capacity for communication.[37] Further, whilst language supplies evidence of that desire, it neither erodes its distinctiveness nor excludes the possibility of such an essentially human impulse finding expression through other means, such as becoming proficient in alternative semiotic systems (e.g. bodily gesture, facial expression, etc.). In a similar way, religious beliefs not only supply a 'language' for faith, but also bear witness to an existential openness and instinct to explore selfhood through being-in-relation – a disposition that exists in dialectical juxtaposition to its correspondent, where beliefs shape the experience of faith and faith informs the content of belief.[38] In a similar vein, Gerd Theissen, in

---

[34] Wilfred Cantwell Smith, *Faith and Belief* (Princeton: Princeton University Press, 1979), 142; also *The Meaning and End of Religion* (Minneapolis, MN: Fortress, 1962), 170–92.

[35] James W. Fowler, *Stages in Faith: The Psychology of Human Development and the Quest for Meaning* (San Francisco: Harper & Row, 1981), 16, 24–5.

[36] For example, Edward J. Hughes in *Wilfred Cantwell Smith: A Theology for the World* (London: SCM, 1986) and Mary Ford-Grabowsky, 'What Developmental Phenomenon Is Fowler Studying?', *Journal of Psychology and Christianity* 5 (1986), 5–13.

[37] The evolution of language continues to be hotly debated. Interestingly, a capacity associated with Broca's Area, usually in the left hemisphere, may have evolved via music within the more relational, synthetic right hemisphere as a means of communication. 'Music is likely to be the ancestor of language and it arose largely in the right hemisphere, where one would expect a means of communication with others, promoting social cohesion, to arise'. Iain McGilchrist, *The Master and His Emissary: The Divided Brain and the Making of the Western World*, new ed. (New Haven, CT: Yale University Press, 2019), 105. McGilchrist goes on to explain how the acquisition of verbal competency, especially referential language, became associated with a shift from right- to left-hemisphere activity and, with that, a greater emphasis upon manipulation of the outside world over personal communication (111–15).

[38] On the reciprocity of faith and belief, Paul Tillich, *Dynamics of Faith* (New York: Harper, 1957), 9–14.

a study of the miracle stories attributed to Jesus in the Gospels, describes faith's 'boundary-crossing' (*grenzüberschreitendes*) function by which exponents reach beyond their socially constructed worlds to embrace a fuller sense of self in relation to that which lies beyond conformity to the presiding belief system.[39]

2.2 Faith

We are persuaded of the basis for and value in distinguishing between *faith* as an inherently human impulse or potentiality towards transcendence and *belief* as the interpretative framework or semiotic system that supplies a vehicle for such exploration. In this distinction, the former can be likened to an ecstatic inclination or, at times, thrust – more often than not, unconscious – beckoning us to explore and expand the contours of our personhood through relating, however tentatively and inchoately, to the 'other' in its many manifestations. For the infant, it motivates the crawl, the cry and the cuddle; for the teenager, the yearning for independence, sexual experimentation and immersive experiences; for the adult, falling in love, procreation and parenthood, employment and role diversification. None of these characterizations is universal or exhaustive, of course – simply instantiations of an existential orientation towards self-transcendence which also, through these and other expressions, possesses the capacity to relate us to the subtle Otherness religious belief systems call God.[40] Whilst not distinguishing between faith and belief, the anthropologist Agustín Fuentes has recently demonstrated how faith's capacity for self-transcendence, for intuiting the unexperienced and investing in it, is necessary in order to account for human evolution and the emergence of what he describes as the human niche:

> Belief is the most prominent, promising, and dangerous capacity that humanity has evolved. Belief is the ability to draw on our range of cognitive and social resources, our histories and experiences, and combine them with our imagination. It is the power to think beyond what is here and now and develop mental representations in order to see and feel and know something – an idea, a vision, a necessity, a possibility, a truth – that is not immediately present to the senses, and then to invest, wholly and authentically, in that 'something' so that it becomes one's reality. Beliefs and belief systems permeate human neurobiologies, bodies, and ecologies, acting as dynamic agents in evolutionary processes. The human capacity for belief, the specifics of belief, and our

---

[39] Gerd Theissen, *Miracle Stories of the Early Christian Tradition*, trans. Francis McDonagh (Edinburgh: T. & T. Clark, 1983), 129–40.

[40] See James Fowler, *Stages of Faith*, especially parts I and III.

diverse belief systems structure and shape our daily lives, our societies, and the world around us. We are human, therefore we believe.[41]

It is important to underline that drawing this distinction between faith and belief invites us to conceive of the former as, to quote Raimon Panikkar, 'a constitutive dimension of man [*sic*]'[42] – one that is ontologically anterior to belief, intrinsically phenomenal in nature and essentially dispositional in character. As such, faith can be thought of as an individuating impulse within each person-in-the-making and one which, at this undifferentiated stage, must be deduced from its inclinations: a sense of incompleteness and yearning or, equally, a sense of fascination and inquisitiveness, or a capacity to imagine the unexperienced, inclining us to reach beyond the safe confines of the self in pursuit of a fuller sense of human being in relation to the other. It should also be noted that this heuristic drive can find expression in journeys within the self as much as journeys beyond, as is the case in what John Bowker refers to as 'inversive' religious systems such as Buddhism where a more authentic sense of self emerges from, for example, discovering one's place within the transitory quality characterizing all that appears to be.[43] Equally, we should stress that faith's authenticity resides in its very essence and potential for human flourishing. Whether this is accomplished is a measure not so much of faith's capacity of itself as in how it finds expression. Again, drawing on an analogy previously employed, whilst it may be impossible to prove the existence of an innate need to communicate from modes of human communication, it is nonetheless a reasonable deduction. Further, this need to communicate endures even though it exposes us to potentially destructive forms of communication. So with faith, whilst its capacity for human flourishing may be frustrated by unsound investment, its existence is not thereby refuted.[44]

It should also be stressed that faith so conceived is not individualistic in its ambitions. Rather, it bears witness to a relational understanding of human being or, more specifically, to a relational ontology in which human beings seek their integrity and fulfilment within complex webs of interrelatedness. In essence, then, faith is a trusting openness to the otherness of being and the being of

---

[41] Agustín Fuentes, *Why We Believe: Evolution and the Human Way of Being* (New Haven, CT: Yale University Press, 2019), ix. Recognition of the foundational role of belief in human evolution does not exclude the possibility of belief also playing a part in the evolution of other species; cf. Alasdair MacIntyre, *Dependent Rational Animals: Why Human Beings Need the Virtues* (London: Duckworth, 1999), esp. 29–41.

[42] Raimon Panikkar, 'Faith: A Constitutive Dimension of Man', *Journal of Ecumenical Studies* 8 (1971), 244.

[43] John Bowker, *Is God a Virus? Genes, Culture and Religion* (London: SPCK, 1995), 155–64.

[44] See H. Richard Niebuhr's discussion of 'broken faith' in *Faith on Earth*, edited posthumously by Richard R. Niebuhr (New Haven, CT: Yale University Press, 1989), 63–82.

others, constituting an existential bridge over which transcendence is encountered, whether in the form of another person, creature or God. Further, although faith finds expression in subjective experience, it is not bound by subjectivity; rather, it is the means for encountering the non-self. At one level, it opens us up and leaves us vulnerable to relationships with other subjects which can be formative in their impact upon our selfhood, whether in a constructive or destructive way. But at a deeper level, faith not only facilitates a particular quality of engagement with, for example, other persons whose existence is manifest to all who care to look, but it also realizes encounter with that sacred Otherness whose presence is subtle and implicit.[45] As such, faith can be conceived as the personal investment by which transcendence crystallizes into immanence within human experience. It does not synthesize the transcendent dimension, but it does actualize it within personal subjectivity.[46]

It is important to clarify what is not being proposed here. Whilst recognizing the important insights from disciplines such as anthropology, neuroscience, phenomenology, psychology, sociology and so forth, we are not commending an exclusively anthropocentric account of religious belief.[47] On the contrary, what we are proposing is that faith is best conceived as an existential orientation which opens us up to the possibility of encountering transcendence, whilst leaving unresolved at this stage the nature and limits of such encounter. What is more, we would also wish to claim that such faith-filled heuristic receptivity can characterize many human relationships of genuine encounter and not just those associated with religious belief, which partially accounts for why there is considerable overlap in the vocabulary of devotion when expressing love between persons and love between persons and God. Hopefully, enough has been said to establish, at least as a working hypothesis, the existence of faith as a phenomenon that, although closely associated with religious belief, is discrete from it and can find expression in other forms of being-in-relation. As such, we

---

[45] 'Faith, selfhood and other-self are inseparable .... The certainty of faith may be stated in a somewhat Cartesian fashion: I believe ... therefore I know that I am, but also I trust you and therefore I am certain that you are, and I trust and distrust the Ultimate Environment, the Absolute Source of my being, therefore I acknowledge that He is. There are three realities of which I am certain, self, companions and the Transcendent'. Niebuhr, *Faith on Earth*, 61.

[46] An analogy from science may help here. The role of measurement and, by implication, of the measurer is crucial when investigating quantum phenomena within the subatomic world of particle physics, where the location of, say, a photon cannot be known precisely when unmeasured and is best represented by a probabilistic wave function. It is only through measurement that the wave function appears to collapse into particularity with the photon gaining position. For a non-technical discussion, Adam Becker, *What Is Real? The Unfinished Quest for the Meaning of Quantum Physics* (London: John Murray, 2018), 13–20.

[47] See the detailed review of John Bowker in *The Sense of God: Sociological, Anthropological and Psychological Approaches to the Origin of the Sense of God* (Oxford: One World, 1995; new preface).

are closer to the truth when we identify faith as a vital constituent of human being and flourishing, rather than as an exclusive prerogative of religious believers.

2.3 Belief Systems

What then of *belief*? Faith, as defined in Section 2.2, is an orientation towards otherness and potentiality for being-in-relation which leads to and finds expression through exploratory investments in particular subjects. These investments are informed by both the perception of the subject and the characteristics of the relationship. This is where belief enters the room. We mentioned previously how belief can be likened to a language supplying a vehicle for self-expression or, in the case of faith, self-transcendence, as well as for communication. As with our mother tongue, where we may have no recollection of attempting to think or express ourselves or communicate prior to the acquisition of language, so those who grew up within a religious tradition will probably have little, if any, awareness of faith apart from the belief system to which they belong. For others, faith may well be the impetus for exploring a religious tradition in the first instance and, where resonances are discerned, explorers may choose subsequently to immerse themselves within it through, for example, participating in worship, belonging to a community, receiving catechesis, serving an apprenticeship and so forth. In other cases again, those born into a religious tradition may at some juncture become aware of a dissonance between their faith and the beliefs through which it seeks expression. Where this occurs, some measure of revision in beliefs, if tolerated within that religious tradition, may be required to restore resonance; if this proves impossible, the exponent may experience what is sometimes described as a loss of faith, although in the light of the distinction drawn in Section 2.2, it would be more correctly classed as a crisis in belief. Where resonance between faith and a belief system can be established, however, then the latter becomes for the former not only a channel for expressing ultimate concern,[48] but also a medium for being-in-relation to the

---

[48] 'The term "ultimate concern" unites the subjective and the objective side of the act of faith – the *fides qua creditur* (the faith through which one believes) and the *fides quae creditur* (the faith which is believed). The first is the classical term for the centered act of the personality, the ultimate concern. The second is the classical term for that toward which this act is directed, the ultimate itself, expressed in symbols of the divine. This distinction is very important, but not ultimately so, for the one side cannot be without the other. There is no faith without a content toward which it is directed. There is always something meant in the act of faith. And there is no way of having the content of faith except in the act of faith. All speaking about divine matters which is not done in the state of ultimate concern is meaningless. Because that which is meant in the act of faith cannot be approached in any other way than through the act of faith'. Tillich, *Dynamics of Faith*, 11–12.

sacred Other which can be, in certain circumstances, two-way as the believer grows in understanding of and learns to live in the presence of the sacred.[49]

We will say more about this process shortly, but before doing so we should clarify what is meant by a *belief system* along with the role of beliefs and the act of believing within it.[50] A belief system constitutes an interpretative environment within which life is experienced. Through sacred texts and holy shrines, religious beliefs and rituals, rules of life and patterns of worship, a symbolic world is constructed that conditions all aspects of living, as well as of interpreting the Other. Unlike beliefs that form an integral part, belief systems are all-pervading yet defy definitive exposition; more often than not, communities of allegiance are their custodians where they are inculcated within and animate the common life of the community through shared worship and practice, as well as through annual cycles of festivals and observances. But more than that, communities not only preserve belief systems, they embody them in the sense that they have no independent existence. In this and other respects, they are comparable in reach to concepts such as culture and worldview – both of which, consciously or unconsciously, shape lived experience and yet, whilst generating artefacts bearing witness to their presence, remain greater than the sum of their parts. The Canadian philosopher Charles Taylor's 'social imaginary' is also a helpful analogue:

> What I am trying to get at with this term is something much broader and deeper than the intellectual schemes people may entertain when they think about social reality in disengaged mode. I am thinking rather of the ways in which they imagine their social existence, how they fit together with others, how things go on between them and their fellows, the expectations which are normally met, and the deeper normative notions and images which underlie these expectations ... I speak of imaginary because I am talking about the way ordinary people imagine their social surroundings, and this is often not expressed in theoretical terms, it is carried in images, stories, legends ... the

---

[49] Again, this approach is congruent with Fowler's stages in faith where the process of human individuation can be charted in terms of growing through certain conceptions of belief as faith seeks a more adequate framework for interpreting experience and engaging with existential challenges. I have explored this in 'Theological Education through the Eyes of Faith Development: Towards a Critical Appraisal', *British Journal of Theological Education* 7 (1995/6), 22–30.

[50] The following works have contributed to the understanding of belief systems offered here: Pierre Bourdieu, *Outline of a Theory of Practice*, trans. Richard Nice (Cambridge: Cambridge University Press, 1977); John Bowker, *Licensed Insanities: Religions and Belief in God in the Contemporary World* (London: DLT, 1987); Roy A. Rappaport, *Ritual and Religion in the Making of Humanity* (Cambridge: Cambridge University Press, 1999); Charles Taylor, *A Secular Age* (Cambridge, MA: Belknap Press of Harvard University Press, 2007); Victor Turner, *The Ritual Process: Structure and Anti-Structure* (New York: Aldine de Gruyter, 1969); Ludwig Wittgenstein, *Philosophical Investigations*, trans. G. E. M. Anscombe (Oxford: Blackwell, 1978).

social imaginary is that common understanding which makes possible common practices and a widely shared sense of legitimacy.[51]

Another important characteristic of belief systems is their self-authenticating nature.[52] In fact, their plausibility tends to be conditional upon participation within communities of allegiance, which represents a natural process of assimilation for those born within such a climate, but is far more challenging for the outsider who may struggle to find various components compelling prior to enculturation. In particular, beliefs can appear incredible or plain nonsense when divorced from their symbolic worlds – in a comparable way to the offside rule in football, the restricted movements of a knight on a chess board or the role of Black Rod in various Commonwealth parliaments. None of these makes any sense in itself, but is furnished with significance within the system to which it belongs, where its meaning becomes clear and its authority unequivocal. Whilst necessarily possessing an internal coherence which resonates with the faith of adherents, many systems of belief employ authoritative figures to reinforce their plausibility, integrity and veracity through teaching, as well as through the performance of key rituals and practices.

It should be pointed out that belief systems, rooted in a priori beliefs whose plausibility is dependent upon the system itself, are by no means restricted to religion. In fact, a good case could be made that most, if not all, fields of human endeavour necessarily deploy them, including scientific inquiry which more often than not appears to take for granted that the universe is real (i.e. not simply an illusion), closed (i.e. not subject to supernatural intervention), contingent (i.e. open to change), rational (i.e. understandable) and predictable or, at least, predictably unpredictable (cf. Heisenberg). None of these can be proven beyond doubt. They are all beliefs. But by adopting them, scientists have been able not only to make sense of many aspects of the physical world, but also to harness its resources. And, in a practical sense, this can be garnered as evidence for such beliefs being true, yet they remain *provisional* and, from time to time, may need to be revised to accommodate previously unaccounted-for phenomena, such as, in science, those characterizing the subatomic quantum world.[53] Further, belief systems, whether scientific or otherwise, are also *partial* in the sense that they

---

[51] Taylor, *A Secular Age*, 171–2.

[52] See Peter Berger's understanding of religions as 'plausibility structures' developed in a number of publications, including Peter L. Berger and Thomas Luckmann, *The Social Construction of Reality: A Treatise in the Sociology of Knowledge* (New York: Doubleday, 1966). Also Thomas Kuhn's discussion of how 'paradigms' function in *The Structure of Scientific Revolutions*, 3rd ed. (Chicago: University of Chicago Press, 1996); Kuhn is particularly strong on the role of communities within paradigms.

[53] See the discussion of Rupert Sheldrake throughout *The Science Delusion: Freeing the Spirit of Enquiry* (London: Coronet, 2012).

only relate us to a subset of human experience and exploration.[54] For example, when evaluating the artistic merit of a Rembrandt masterpiece, we would be unlikely to make much progress by carrying out X-ray spectroscopy or Carbon-14 dating. Equally, it is highly doubtful that research into the nature of consciousness will be advanced simply by analysing the brain's chemical constituents or electrical activity.

2.4 Beliefs

And what of the role of *beliefs* within a religious belief system? They tend to supply the anatomy for the performance of faith within such a system – delimiting group identity, shaping worship, informing ethical conduct and defining life-goals. For example, monotheistic belief can constitute a prerequisite to participation in a particular believing community, demanding that worship be focused exclusively on the one true God, whilst framing all other forms of devotion as idolatrous and beckoning believers to dedicate themselves to divine service. Such commitments and practices would lack plausibility or persuasion without an underlying monotheistic belief; equally, the underlying belief would be, in terms of human being, meaningless without practical application. As the author of the Epistle of James memorably affirmed: 'You believe that God is one; you do well. Even the demons believe – and shudder . . .. For just as the body without the spirit is dead, so faith without works is also dead' (2.19, 26). Or expressed slightly differently, monotheistic belief is barren without embodied faith: orthodoxy and orthopraxy are essentially connected.

In the light of this, is the priority of faith over belief advocated earlier in this section sustainable? Yes, but with qualification. If faith is an orientation towards otherness and potentiality for being-in-relation which leads to and finds expression through concrete investments in particular subjects, then beliefs supply a characterization of the other with whom we are drawn into relationship. Where the subject of transcendence is another person, this characterization, which remains dynamic and provisional, is informed primarily by personal experience and aspiration, supported by data gleaned from other sources such as the testimony of a third party or reputational information. However, where the subject is the divine, characterization tends to take the form of inherited beliefs about the deity which, as we have seen, can be embodied within

---

[54] I am aware this claim is incompatible with various schools of thought. For example, if you believe that only entities open to empirical investigation are real or that everything can be explained in terms of physical interactions, then whatever falls outside these definitions becomes invisible or is simply ignored. See the critique of David Bentley Hart in *Atheist Delusions: The Christian Revolution and Its Fashionable Enemies* (New Haven, CT: Yale University Press, 2009).

Scripture or formulated into creeds, although they can also be communicated more indirectly and subtly through devotional materials such as hymns, prayers, liturgical practices and rules of life. Initially, these are taken on trust, providing an introductory framework for encounter, but as noted previously, they are subsequently measured against personal experience, reflection and reasoning – an ongoing, dialectical process in which a believer explores whether beliefs resonate with experience or supply a convincing interpretation of it. For example, a believer may be satisfied that monotheism accounts for why there is something rather than nothing, whilst also providing a plausible explanation for that person's experience of, to borrow Rudolf Otto's phrase, *mysterium tremendum et fascinans*.[55]

We should also note that whilst a case can be made for maintaining that faith as an individuating impulse is a universal constituent of human being, what the act of believing entails is open to variation in space and time. In his book, *Belief and History*, Wilfred Cantwell Smith examines how the semantic content of the language of belief has shifted through the ages. Strikingly, he summarizes the transition thus:

> Indeed, one might perhaps sum up one aspect of the history of these matters over the past few centuries in the following way. The affirmation 'I believe in God' used to mean: 'Given the reality of God as a fact of the universe, I hereby pledge to Him my heart and soul. I committedly opt to live in loyalty to Him. I offer my life to be judged by Him, trusting His mercy'. To-day the statement may be taken by some as meaning: 'Given the uncertainty as to whether there be a God or not, as a fact of modern life, I announce that my opinion is "yes". I judge God to be existent'.[56]

Underpinning this change is a far-reaching revision in the pervading social imaginary (cf. Charles Taylor) – shaping experience, informing judgement and determining allegiances – a vital component of which are the implicit beliefs and assumptions which, for the most part, are taken for granted.[57] Prior to the rise of humanism and the European Enlightenment, for instance, the existence of God was rarely questioned publicly in the Christian West (or, indeed, in many other parts of the world), not least because there was no recognized authority

---

[55] It is conceivable that faith and belief are the prerogative of the brain's two cerebral hemispheres, with the latter emerging from the left's capacity for focused attention, lending itself to analysis and conceptualization of the already recognized, and the former emerging from the right's capacity for alertness, sustained attention and vigilance, lending itself to exploration and openness to fresh experience. See McGilchrist's discussion of the different characteristics of the hemispheres in *Master and His Emissary*, 33–49.

[56] Wilfred Cantwell Smith, *Belief and History* (Charlottesville, VA: Virginia University Press, 1977), 44.

[57] Taylor, *Secular Age*, esp. 171–6.

capable of doing so. However, with the elevation of reason to above or at least on a par with Scripture and the papal magisterium, what was once assumed as a given became an object of scrutiny, exposed to rational evaluation. Furthermore, with the arbiter of truth translocating from the Roman Catholic Church and its Princes to the minds of thinking individuals (cf. *cogito ergo sum*, Rene Descartes), even God becomes a matter of opinion. Accompanying this epistemological revolution, according to Smith, belief ceases to be a subjective investment of trust and allegiance in the givenness of God and takes the form of intellectual assent to the proposition of whether or not God exists. What is more, within secular democracies, such believing is a manifestation of non-conformity, deviancy from the presiding social imaginary, which can only be tolerated so long as the consequences of believing are compatible with the liberties of other citizens – a balancing act currently preoccupying many Western administrations.[58]

This shift in the meaning of believing in God brings into focus the distinction between *implicit and explicit beliefs*. Within a theocentric social imaginary, the existence of the divine is an implicit belief which is assumed rather than consciously embraced; further, it is one that supplies the springboard for explicit belief in the form of personal allegiance and commitment, which would be altogether more demanding without the assurance of God's permanency – God's existence beyond human subjectivity. By contrast, within an anthropo-centric imaginary, the implicit beliefs of science and secularism have forced belief in God into the domain of explicit belief with at least three consequences. First, the opinionizing of God's existence severs the link between orthodoxy and orthopraxy – it is perfectly possible to believe there is a God whilst concurrently living as if there isn't. Second, believers who do choose to pledge allegiance to God and live accordingly have to make the prior investment of belief in whether or not there is a God in whom to believe. This is substantially more challenging, as the following illustration elucidates. If I was to ask, 'Do you believe in Ian Wallis?', you are most likely to interpret this question along the lines of whether or not you would be willing to entrust yourself to him, believing him to be trustworthy. However, when the existence of Ian Wallis itself becomes a matter of personal belief, then the task of entrusting yourself to

---

[58] This forms one of the arguments of the so-called new atheism position, namely that religious beliefs are dangerous because they inform and inspire antisocial, sometimes life-endangering, behaviour; e.g. Sam Harris, *The End of Faith: Religion, Terror and the Future of Reason* (New York: W. W. Norton, 2004). However, this critique relates principally to fundamentalism, rather than to religion per se. Whilst there are religious fundamentalists who claim to perpetrate acts of terror in the name of their god, it is questionable whether religious beliefs motivate or justify such behaviour; further, and more importantly, by far the majority of religious believers are not motivated by their beliefs to act in this way.

someone whose very being is contingent upon your prior subjective appropriation is wholly more problematic – which underlines the importance of belief systems, animated by believing communities, where God's existence is restored to the realm of implicit belief, of that which can be assumed.

Third, shifting God's existence from implicit to explicit has the effect of privatizing religious belief as alternative narratives within the pervading social imaginary are constructed to account for the universe and our place within it. This has wide-ranging implications, encompassing many aspects of life – from the grounds of national identity to the rationale for monarchies, from the basis for morality to the teaching of science, from the swearing of oaths to the contents of funerals. Further, whilst religions have always offered believers an alternative sense of self, the bracketing of religious communities along with other groups of non-conformity requires that adherents embrace a form of self-induced schizophrenia in which they must convincingly inhabit different identities informed by mutually incompatible imaginaries.[59]

2.5 Believing

So far in this section we have attempted to build a case for distinguishing faith from belief, before moving on to explore the nature and function of belief systems and beliefs within those systems. Next, we turn our attention to the *act of believing* which, in the light of these findings, can be defined as an investment of faith in the subject of belief – in this case, God. The grounds for making such an investment of the self are potentially multifarious. For instance, where belief systems are inherited, the act of believing can be appropriated through assimilation. In other cases, it may result from being persuaded by the reasonableness or appeal of a belief system or by the testimony of already practising exponents or by an animating community. Or, again, personal experience may be the driving force as believing emerges as a suitable, even compelling, response. However arrived at, the act of believing, especially in the early stages, entails risk and the prospect of personal diminishment – because, whatever the grounds for belief, they are never beyond doubt;[60] yet, paradoxically, as we shall explain shortly, the only truly convincing confirmation that such an investment of faith is well placed necessarily emerges retrospectively. In this

---

[59] Self-evidently, this is a demanding undertaking, as is illustrated by those occasions when the demands of one identity conflict with those of another as, for example, occurred for some Muslims living in Western democracies when a fatwa was issued against Salman Rushdie following the publication of his fictional novel, *The Satanic Verses* (London: Penguin, 1988); see the discussion of Kenan Malik in *From Fatwa to Jihad: The Rushdie Affair and Its Legacy* (London: Atlantic Books, 2009).

[60] On the role of doubt within belief, see Anthony Thiselton, *Doubt, Faith, and Certainty* (Grand Rapids, MI: Eerdmans, 2017), 37–58.

respect, the act of believing in God shares commonalities with similar acts of belief – from fifteenth-century maritime explorers acquiring the wherewithal before sailing into the unknown in search of the so-called New World, to twenty-first-century subatomic physicists persuading their financiers to construct the Large Hadron Collider at CERN before performing experiments in the hope of demonstrating the existence of the Higgs Field. There may have been no New World. The Higgs Field and its associated particle, the Higgs Boson, may have been a flawed hypothesis. In each case, there was no way of finding out without the prior act of belief and being exposed to its attendant risks.

As we argued earlier, where secular, anthropocentric social imaginaries hold sway, the act of believing in God requires an acknowledgement of a God in whom to believe. In some cases, this may be as far as believing goes, without the adoption of a particular belief system and its associated implications for living – thereby minimizing risk, but also the prospect of verification, in a similar way to how someone may believe in the healing properties of acupuncture without ever putting them to the test. Where the act of believing extends beyond expressing an opinion on God's existence to embracing a belief system, then the investment of faith is more far-reaching. For one thing, it is likely to entail the adoption of qualifying beliefs which attribute to the divine certain characteristics (e.g. God is love, righteous and holy; God is omnipotent, omniscient and omnipresent, etc.) and commitments (e.g. God creates and sustains the universe; God seeks humanity's cooperation in covenant; God's purposes for creation will be fulfilled, etc.). For another, the act of believing will extend beyond intellectual assent to include behavioural and affectional responses to living in relation to the God so characterized in the aforementioned beliefs, including attitudes, conduct and priorities. Broadly speaking, the act of believing entails committing to living a manner of life that is at least compatible with a belief system, if not one that expounds it. Central to this undertaking is worship – the attributing of worth to the God who is believed in. In the broadest sense, this encompasses the entirety of human response to the divine, but within most religious belief systems narrower definitions can also be found where worship denotes some form of devotion to or adoration of the sacred.[61] This highlights the essentially personal nature of believing, both in the sense that it involves the person as a whole, but also that it orientates the believer to the divine in a personal way.

This latter observation needs further clarification. Our discussion of God's being or essence, including whether it is meaningful to describe God as

---

[61] See the survey of the major religions edited by Jean Holm with John Bowker in *Worship* (London: Pinter, 1994).

a person, awaits us in a later section. At this juncture, we wish to make a different point by drawing attention to a defining characteristic within the human orientation towards the divine – of how we relate to God. As the Jewish philosopher, Martin Buber, convincingly demonstrated in *I and Thou*, God is knowable or relatable to not as an object, as an 'it', but as a subject, a 'thou'.[62] This has important implications for the status of faith and believing within the divine–human relationship in the sense that it establishes them as the principal mode of human relating, not because they must serve as a second best in the absence of more supposedly 'scientific' channels of investigation or knowing, but because they reflect that nature of the Other who is being related to. Relating to God, to draw on a previous illustration, cannot be likened to proving the existence of the Higgs Field. There is no apparatus, however sophisticated, that could be designed to isolate God; no experiment, however ingenious, capable of distilling divine essence; no computation, however complex, possessing the potential to resolve the God conundrum. Not because God is very elusive, but because God is not objectifiable in this manner – any more than is, say, the love characterizing human relating. If someone in a committed relationship attempted to prove a partner's love by employing a private investigator to ensure that a third party wasn't involved, then that very act would undermine, if not destroy, the only genuine channel by which confirmation could flow, namely a trusting relating to that person, a living 'as if'. In a similar way, the canons of personal relating are the most appropriate medium for divine encounter.

Further, as it is only when couples trust one another, believing in a partner's love and attempting to live in its light, that they can gauge whether such commitments ring true, so it is through investing the self in trusting openness to the divine Other and living 'as if' the God so believed in actually *is* that the faith-full are able to assess whether such an orientation is well founded, resonating with experience whilst engendering fruitful engagement with those existential challenges characterizing the human condition, such as why we are here, what life is for, where we are heading and how we should live. It is in this sense that relating to God can be conceived of as two-way. Putting to one side for a moment the possibility of supernatural revelation in which God responds when beckoned or takes the initiative unbidden, where faith's investment of the self through believing in God yields an enrichment of, or an expansiveness within, a person's quality of human being as outlined earlier in the section, there may be grounds for concluding that this resulting condition constitutes a kind of

---

[62] Martin Buber, *I and Thou*, trans. Walter Kaufmann (Edinburgh: T. & T. Clark, 1970).

response and one that can develop through time in the light of fresh experience, reflection and existential challenge.

At this point, it may be questioned how such alleged 'feedback' differs from wishful thinking. That is to say, how can we be confident that believing in God relates us to anything beyond the notion of God so conceived within those beliefs? Given that God seems to be beyond the reaches of scientific inquiry, evidence is most likely to be found among the effects of believing on the life of the believer. Here we need to return to relational ontology which was introduced earlier in the section and to the hypothesis that relations between entities are not only as ontologically fundamental as the entities themselves, but are also inherently constitutive of them.[63] At a supra-atomic level, where materiality appears to be self-evident, this seems highly questionable; however, at a subatomic level, where matter dissolves into interactions between wave-like particles which only gain location and mass when observed, relational ontology may well offer a more persuasive account of the essential nature of the physical universe than substantivist alternatives. Further, the centrality of relationships within the construction of identity and selfhood is emphasized in the personalist anthropologies of Martin Buber, John MacMurray and many others, suggesting that it is only within a web of interrelatedness that human potentiality is realized.[64] From this perspective, relationships with others are essential to human being with the capacity to affect us for good or ill. For example, a child whose upbringing is devoid of loving relationships is unlikely to form a self-image of a lovable person who is capable of love. Equally, gifted students who are taught by inspirational educators are more likely to excel than those denied such input and stimuli.[65] In a comparable way, if believing in God engenders human flourishing, or yields fresh insights into the meaning of existence, or unlocks reserves of hope and endurance, or supplies a previously unrealized capacity for forgiveness, or simply makes life worth living, then would this not constitute evidence of a kind of transcendent Other, of a subject of belief, whose immanence is instantiated within the effects of believing on the believer?

---

[63] An interdisciplinary exploration of relational ontology can be found in John Polkinghorne (ed.), *The Trinity and an Entangled World: Relationality in Physical Science and Theology* (Grand Rapids, MI: Eerdmans, 2010).

[64] For example, Martin Buber, *I and Thou* and John MacMurray, *Persons in Relation* (New York: Humanity Books, 1999; original 1961); see also Alistair I. McFadyen, *The Call to Personhood* (Cambridge: Cambridge University Press, 1990) and John D. Zizioulas, *Being as Communion* (London: DLT, 1985).

[65] See the work on 'attachment and loss' theory pioneered by John Bowlby and summarized in *The Making and Breaking of Affectional Bonds* (London: Tavistock/Routledge, 1979).

To expect a higher level of demonstration would be to misunderstand the epistemological constraints of the exploration and to do so by committing a category error with respect to the nature of divine being. Whilst not wishing to pre-empt the findings of future sections, whoever or whatever is denoted by the epithet God as an Other transcending human subjectivity cannot be an entity within space-time – a *daimon* or demiurge in ancient parlance – possessing properties open in principle to empirical investigation.[66] God isn't a hypothesis that is falsifiable in a Popperian sense;[67] however, believing in God can be thought of as an existential experiment and one that is, in principle, both repeatable and capable of eliciting reproducible results in terms of the effects of believing on a believer. Again, a partial analogy from science: the existence of black holes, which cannot be observed directly owing to the magnitude of their gravitational fields, must be inferred from their effects on matter, such as stars, or electromagnetic radiation, including light – both of which are drawn into a black hole's vortex once the event horizon has been crossed.[68] Could not a similar 'effects' approach be adopted with respect to God?

A not unreasonable question to raise at this juncture would be why other 'proofs' for the existence of God haven't been marshalled in support of our case based on personal experience. In a contemporary restatement of some of the classic formulations, Edward Feser offers the following summary:

> The Aristotelian proof begins with the fact that there are potentialities that are actualized and argues that we cannot make sense of this unless we affirm the existence of something which can actualize the potential existence of things without itself being actualized, a *purely actual actualizer*. The neo-Platonic proof begins with the fact that the things of our experience are composed of parts and argues that such things could not exist unless they have an *absolutely simple or noncomposite cause*. The Augustinian proof begins with the fact that there are abstract objects like universals, propositions, numbers, and possible worlds, and argues that these must exist as ideas in a *divine intellect*. The Thomistic proof begins with the real distinction, in each of the things of our experience, between its essence and its existence, and argues that the ultimate cause of such things must be something which is *subsistent existence itself*. The rationalist proof begins with the principle of sufficient reason and argues that the ultimate explanation of things can only lie in an *absolutely necessary being*.[69]

---

[66] On this point, see the convincing account of David Bentley Hart, *The Experience of God: Being, Consciousness, Bliss* (New Haven, CT: Yale University Press, 2013), 35–7, 87–151.

[67] On Karl Popper's principle of falsification, see Adam Becker, *What Is Real?*, 260–4.

[68] I have drawn here on the description of black holes offered by the theoretical physicist Carlo Rovelli in *Reality Is Not What It Seems: The Journey to Quantum Gravity*, trans. Simon Carnell and Erica Segre (London: Penguin, 2017), 195–201.

[69] Edward Feser, *Five Proofs of the Existence of God* (San Francisco: Ignatius, 2017), 169, italics original.

We would argue that these and similar demonstrations of God's existence through logic and reason can constitute valuable antecedents to personal believing by supplying intellectually robust grounds, especially within imaginaries where God's existence is no longer a matter of implicit belief. They can also, as we shall note shortly, supply explicatory capacity to monotheistic belief. However, their assent cannot be equated with, nor does it often result in, personal believing in the fullest sense outlined earlier, because, like certain forms of mathematical proof where, given predefined axioms and criteria, the resolution of a particular equation can be intellectually compelling, logical necessity need have no correlate in existential reality or engender a corresponding investment of faith.[70] For example, I can acknowledge that the universe requires a 'purely actual actualizer' to account for its existence without it making one jot of difference to how I choose to live my life.

3 The Status of Religious Beliefs

In the previous section, we proposed that faith is an individuating impulse orientating us towards transcendence – towards encountering the mysterious otherness which is beyond our immediate sense of self. We also proposed that religious belief systems supply an all-embracing interpretative framework within which faith's existential openness can be owned, expressed, explored and, hopefully, to some measure, fulfilled in relation to the divine – usually within the context of a believing community whose constitution and vocation is to preserve, embody and evolve the belief system in question. Within this scenario, beliefs supply a belief system's anatomy, providing structure and form, as well as rationale and meaning, boundaries and a sense of identity. In this section, we will examine the status of religious beliefs, especially beliefs in relation to God.

3.1 The Nature of Beliefs

To help gain perspective, our point of departure will be the analysis of doctrinal formulations offered by the American Lutheran theologian George Lindbeck in his seminal book, *The Nature of Doctrine*. Lindbeck's contribution emerges from an ecumenical context and the pursuit of a paradigm which creates the 'possibility of doctrinal reconciliation without capitulation'.[71] Before advancing his own thesis, he outlines two others which he describes in these terms:

---

[70] See the discussion of John Bowker in *Licensed Insanities*, 50–1.
[71] George Lindbeck, *The Nature of Doctrine: Religion and Theology in a Postliberal Age* (Philadelphia: Westminster, 1984), 16.

The *Cognitive-Propositional* 'emphasizes the cognitive aspects of religion and stresses the ways in which church doctrines function as informative propositions or truth claims about objective realities'.

The *Experiential-Expressive* 'interprets doctrines as noninformative and nondiscursive symbols of inner feelings, attitudes, or existential orientations ... highlights the resemblances of religions to aesthetic enterprises'. (16)

In addition, he adumbrates a mediating third way, the *Cognitive-Experiential*, where '[b]oth the cognitively propositional and the expressively symbolic dimensions and functions of religions and doctrines are viewed, at least in the case of Christianity, as religiously significant and valid' (16).

According to Lindbeck, all three fail his canon of 'doctrinal reconciliation without capitulation'. In the case of cognitive-propositional approaches, doctrine enshrines truth claims which cannot be relativized with the consequence that, where mutually incompatible doctrines are held (e.g. different understandings of Christ's eucharistic presence), only one can be correct at the expense of the others. In the case of experiential-expressive approaches, doctrines fulfil a symbolic function, engendering or expressing the feelings, attitudes, existential orientations and aspirations of believers. As such, they are malleable and polyvalent, providing no stable core of meaning for ecumenical dialogue whilst potentially shrouding areas of commonality. Lindbeck is more sympathetic towards the Cognitive-Experiential approaches of Karl Rahner and Bernard Lonergan, recognizing that they are better equipped 'to account more fully than can the first two types for both variable and invariable aspects of religious traditions'. However, in the end they fail his ecumenical test because they have 'difficulty in coherently combining them' and, as a consequence, 'resort to complicated intellectual gymnastics and to that extent are unpersuasive' (17). Lindbeck then proceeds to outline his preferred 'rule-based' *Cultural-Linguistic* paradigm which is informed by insights from the fields of anthropology and sociology, where religion is likened to a language and, together with its correlative form of life, to a culture, and where doctrines serve neither as expressive symbols nor as truth claims, but as 'communally authoritative rules of discourse, attitude, and action' (17).

3.2 Expressive, Interpretative and Formative Beliefs

When published in 1984, *The Nature of Doctrine* generated a great deal of debate, and it continues to serve as a reference point for further discussion. From our perspective, Lindbeck brings into focus four possible dimensions to doctrine and religious beliefs more broadly: the referential, the expressive, the interpretative and the formative. As we shall see, these are not necessarily mutually exclusive and there are clearly areas of symbiosis and overlap; however, one of the key questions that must be addressed later in this section is how the final three relate to the first. Before doing so, we will take a brief excursion into the expressive, interpretative and formative functions of belief.

Consider the opening lines of the so-called Apostles' Creed, 'I believe in God, the Father almighty, creator of heaven and earth'. Notwithstanding the privileged role of creeds within belief systems, this affirmation enshrines belief in an all-powerful creating deity. From an expressive perspective, such a belief can articulate a 'feeling of absolute dependence' which, according to Friedrich Schleiermacher, is constitutive of our self-consciousness, emerging from its 'non-self-caused' (*ein Sichselbstnichtsogesetzthaben*) component – its 'having-by-some-means-come-to-be' (*ein Irgendwiegewordensein*). Schleiermacher explains it thus:

> As regards the stated definitions themselves, it is quite clear that our feeling of absolute dependence could not refer to the universal condition of all finite being if anything in it (i.e. that being) were independent of God or ever had been. It is just as certain that if there could be anything in the whole of finite existence as such which entered into it at its origin independently of God, then because it must exist in us to, the feeling of absolute dependence could have no truth even in relation to ourselves. But if, on the other hand, we think of God the Creator in any way as limited, and thus in His activity resembling that which should be absolutely dependent on him, then the feeling expressing this dependence likewise could not be true (since equality and dependence neutralize each other), and thus the finite in that it resembled God could not to be absolutely dependent upon Him. But except in one of these two forms, a contradiction between any theory of creation and the universal basis of our religious self-consciousness is not conceivable.[72]

Our intention here is not to evaluate Schleiermacher's analysis, but simply to offer it as an example of *expressive belief* where its origin or impetus resides within the believer and that person's need to give expression to, in this case, a 'non-self-caused' sense of being.

Interpretative belief is closely allied to this approach where the emphasis falls on making sense of the human condition. The German-American philosopher and theologian Paul Tillich's method of correlation, where Christian symbols, including beliefs, address the existential challenges of life, is a particularly good case in point, as the following excerpt from his *Systematic Theology* illustrates:

> The doctrine of creation is not the story of an event which took place 'once upon a time'. It is the basic description of the relation between God and the

---

[72] Friedrich Schleiermacher, *The Christian Faith*, trans. H. R. Mackintosh and J. S. Stewart (Edinburgh: T. & T. Clark, 1928), 151–2; see also 12–18.

world. It is the correlate to the analysis of man's finitude. It answers the question implied in man's finitude and in finitude generally. In giving this answer, it discovers that the meaning of finitude is creatureliness. The doctrine of creation is the answer to the question implied in the creature as creature. The question is asked continually and is always answered in man's essential nature.[73]

Again, as previously, beliefs emerge from some aspect of the human condition and, in this case, give an account for it. Equally, as with expressive beliefs, the veracity of interpretative beliefs resides principally in their adequacy in addressing the existential questions or challenges from which they arose.

Formative beliefs, on the other hand, go one step further. Rather than attempting to give expression to or offer an interpretation for some dimension of human being, they supply a hermeneutical framework within which life can be experienced in a particular way, which brings us back to George Lindbeck and his cultural-linguistic stance:

> Stated more technically, a religion can be viewed as a kind of cultural and/or linguistic framework or medium that shapes the entirety of life and thought …. It is not primarily an array of beliefs about the true and the good (though it may involve these), or a symbolism expressive of basic attitudes, feelings, or sentiments (though these will be generated). Rather, it is similar to an idiom that makes possible the description of realities, the formulation of beliefs, and the experiencing of inner attitudes, feelings, and sentiments. Like a culture or language, it is a communal phenomenon that shapes the subjectivities of individuals rather than being primarily a manifestation of those subjectivities. It comprises a vocabulary of discursive and nondiscursive symbols together with a distinctive logic or grammar in terms of which this vocabulary can be meaningfully deployed. Lastly, just as a language (or 'language game', to use Wittgenstein's phrase) is correlated with a form of life, and just as a culture has both cognitive and behavioural dimensions, so it is also in the case of a religious tradition. Its doctrines, cosmic stories or myths, and ethical directives are integrally related to the rituals it practices, the sentiments or experiences it evokes, the actions it recommends, and the institutional forms it develops. (33)

In this case, doctrinal beliefs as rules are generative of lived experience, to be interpreted afresh and embodied within the life of a community – and are, in turn, communicated through and reinforced by the narratives, practices, rituals and attitudes characterizing the religion in question. Although Lindbeck doesn't address belief in a creator God directly, a cultural-linguistic approach is likely to include exploring ways in which a believing community might embody the

---

[73] Paul Tillich, *Systematic Theology: Reason and Revelation, Being and God*, volume 1 (Chicago: University of Chicago Press, 1951), 252.

gratuitousness of existence in its worship, common life and discipleship or inform a response to the current environmental crisis. There are a number of resonances here between Lindbeck's understanding of doctrinal beliefs and the approach adopted in the previous section towards beliefs more generally – for example, their formative, identity-creating and communicative capacities. We would also wish to recognize, contra Lindbeck, their expressive and interpretative functions in certain instances, as we shall see. However, his reticence to entertain doctrinal beliefs as articulations relating to something beyond human subjectivity begs at least two questions which are not satisfactorily addressed.

3.3 Referential Beliefs

Alister McGrath, in his response to Lindbeck, *The Genesis of Doctrine*, levels the following criticism:

> Doctrine, then, describes the regulatory language of the Christian idiom. But how did this language come into being, and to what, if anything, does it refer? Lindbeck appears to suggest that the cultural-linguistic approach to doctrine may dispense with the question of whether the Christian idiom has any external referent. Doctrine is concerned with the internal regulation of the Christian idiom, ensuring its consistency. The question of how that idiom relates to the external world is considered to be improper. For Lindbeck, doctrine is the language of a Christian community, a self-perpetuating idiolect. Indeed, at points he seems to suggest that conceiving theology as the grammar of the Christian language entails the abandonment of any talk about God as an independent reality and any suggestion that it is possible to make truth claims (in an ontological, rather than intrasystemic, sense) concerning him. 'Truth' is firmly equated with – virtually to the point of being reduced to – internal consistency.[74]

If doctrinal beliefs are formative of human experience, rather than simply expressive or interpretative of it, then how did they come into being? What is their origin? This, in turn, elicits a second question: if beliefs possess a certain generative capacity and, with that, an anteriority over experience, do they correlate to anything beyond human experience, such as God? This moves us on to *referential belief* – for what many forms of expressive, interpretative and formative beliefs share in common is at best an agnosticism towards, if not an outright rejection of, theological realism. By contrast, referential beliefs purport to communicate something about the nature or qualities of the Other encountered through faith's self-transcending explorations. As we have seen, Lindbeck struggles with what he describes as cognitive-propositional approaches

---

[74] Alister E. McGrath, *The Genesis of Doctrine: A Study in the Foundation of Doctrinal Criticism* (Grand Rapids, MI: Eerdmans, 1990), 28–9.

because, within the ecumenical context of his project, they fail his 'doctrinal reconciliation without capitulation' rule. Whether this test should be determinative here is debatable, but what makes the situation artificially problematic is his restricted understanding of the 'informative propositions and truth claims about objective realities' doctrines purportedly enshrine. Admittedly, doctrinal beliefs, such as monotheism, tend to be unequivocal in their claims and comprehensive in their reach, rendering alternative beliefs (e.g. polytheism) incompatible – although, as Christianity demonstrates, monotheistic belief can be interpreted in fresh ways. But, more generally, McGrath's criticism of Lindbeck's stance on referential belief is well founded:

> Lindbeck attributes an unmerited inflexibility to cognitive approaches to doctrine through playing down the notion of 'relative adequacy' of doctrinal statements, where 'adequacy' can be assessed both in terms of the original context of a doctrinal formulation and whatever referent it is alleged to represent . . .. Theology is recognized to be concerned with the clarification of the manner in which affirmations about God are, in the first place, derived, and in the second place, how they relate to analogous affirmations drawn from the more familiar world of the senses . . .. Underlying such attempts to achieve clarity of concepts and modes of discourse is the recognition that doctrinal affirmations are to be recognized as perceptions, not total descriptions, pointing beyond themselves towards the greater mystery of God himself . . .. Cognitive theories presuppose use of the non-literal 'four master tropes' of thought and discourse (metaphor, metonymy, synecdoche and irony) in the process of conceptual thinking, rather than reducing them to a crudely literal conception of representation, as Lindbeck seems to suggest . . .. It is necessary to make a clear distinction between the view that an exhaustive and unambiguous account of God is transmitted conceptionally by presuppositions on the one hand, and the view that there is a genuinely cognitive dimension, component or element to doctrinal statements on the other. (16–18, 20)

McGrath goes on to outline four theses about the nature of doctrine which emerge from diachronic analysis of its role within the life of the church:

(1) Doctrine as *social demarcation*: 'a means of creating a sense of social identity, shaping the outlook of a community and justifying its original and continued existence in the face of rival communities with comparable claims' (38).

(2) Doctrine as *interpretation of narrative*: 'The narrative of Jesus Christ, mediated through scripture and eucharistic celebration, is presented, proclaimed *and accepted* as the foundational and controlling narrative of the community of faith . . .. Doctrine provides the conceptual framework by which the scriptural narrative is interpreted . . . [it] articulates the particular interpretation, or range of interpretations, of the

scriptural narrative appropriate to the self-understanding of the Christian community, calling others into question' (55, 58–9).

(3) Doctrine as *interpretation of experience*: 'In order for my experience to be expressed, communicated to or aroused in another, it demands statement in cognitive forms. That these cognitive forms fail to capture such an experience in its totality is self-evident . . . . Doctrine also provides a conceptual apparatus by which the provisional intimations of reality provided by experience may be interpreted and criticised . . . .. In such manners, doctrine is able to address, interpret and transform human experience, correlating it with the parameters of the Christian proclamation' (70–1).

(4) Doctrine as *truth claim*: '[T]here is an ineradicable cognitive element to Christian doctrine, considered as an historical phenomenon. It purports to be a representation, however inadequate or provisional, of the way things really are, in response to the questions arising from the history of Jesus of Nazareth' (75).

Whilst there is considerable common ground between the first and third of these – plus, to a lesser extent, the second – and Lindbeck's cultural-linguistic position, when it comes to the fourth, McGrath wishes to push much further, although with a more nuanced and qualified appreciation of the truth claims doctrines enshrine. It should be stressed at this juncture that he offers an account of Christian doctrine in particular. This is key because Jesus of Nazareth not only supplies a historical reference point for doctrine, but also elicits a raft of questions and phenomena needing to be addressed: 'It is Jesus of Nazareth who precipitates the questions, the process of reflection and construction, which eventually leads to doctrinal formulations' (75). Drawing on insights from Alasdair MacIntrye into the tradition-boundedness of all human inquiry and the impossibility of adopting a 'universal tradition-independent vantage point from which the "rationality" of traditions may be evaluated' (192), he proceeds to demonstrate how doctrines such as the Incarnation make explicit not only what is implicit within the scriptural narrative, but also what emerged within Christian community as it sought to account for Jesus of Nazareth and for his continuing impact within the life of the church and its members. McGrath readily acknowledges that the truthfulness of these doctrines is inaccessible outside of the interpretative tradition and the constituting, custodial community within which they arose; however, he is equally persuaded that such tradition-boundedness characterizes all attempts to account for that which is believed to exist beyond subjective experience and is not peculiar to theology. As a consequence, just as modern history makes truth claims about events which it claims took place in the past and physical science makes truth claims about how the universe really is, so Christian doctrines make truth claims about the God of Jesus of Nazareth:

> Christian doctrine claims to possess significant insights concerning, for example, the character of God and human nature and destiny. Implicit within these truth claims, however, is a subordinate claim: that they are mediated through, perhaps even instantiated in, the person of Jesus of Nazareth. There is, in other words, an implicit Christological reference within the truth claims of Christian doctrine. In declaring that 'God is Love', for example, I am not merely declaring my allegiance to a community that affirms that 'God is Love', irrespective of what God may actually be like. Nor am I merely affirming a broad positive personal attitude to God, irrespective of what he may actually be like. I am affirming that I understand 'God is love' to be an authentic and valid insight into the character of God, and that this belief is grounded, and the hitherto undefined concept of 'love' implicated therein is instantiated, in the history of Jesus of Nazareth. (75)

As noted, McGrath accepts that the truth claims being affirmed here lack persuasiveness outside of their respective interpretative traditions, but that is not so much a weakness as a recognition of how things necessarily are, given there is no unmediated access to that which is believed to be beyond experience. This insight resides at the centre of the Hungarian-British polymath Michael Polanyi's approach in his seminal work, *Personal Knowledge*, in which he demonstrates both the centrality of personal commitment within truth claims about the world beyond experience and, with that, an acknowledgement of their universal reach:

> No one can know universal intellectual standards except by acknowledging their jurisdiction over himself as part of the terms on which he holds himself responsible for the pursuit of his mental efforts. I can speak of facts, knowledge, proof, reality, etc., within my commitment situation, for it is constituted by my search for facts, knowledge, proof, reality, etc., as binding on me. These are proper designations for commitment targets which apply so long as I am committed to them; but they cannot be referred to non-committally. You cannot speak without self-contradiction of knowledge you do not believe, or of a reality which does not exist. I may deny validity to some particular knowledge, or some particular facts, but then to me these are only allegations of knowledge or facts, and should be denoted as 'knowledge' and as 'facts', to which I am not committed. Commitment is in this sense the only path for approaching the universally valid.[75]

---

[75] Michael Polanyi, *Personal Knowledge: Towards a Post-Critical Philosophy* (London: Routledge & Kegan Paul, 1958), 303.

Although I don't think Polanyi coined the phrase, 'believing with universal intent' seems an apt description of McGrath's approach in which not only is subjectivity embraced as a necessary component of truth claims about God (as, indeed, about anything purportedly beyond human experience), but also that such claims entail personal commitment to their veracity and, with that, a recognition of their truthfulness transcending subjectivity, relating the believer to that which is beyond self. Hence the importance of participating experientially within an interpretative tradition in order to discover the truthfulness of Christian doctrinal belief. Whilst McGrath builds his case around the phenomenon of Jesus of Nazareth and the questions his life, death and resurrection elicited, underpinning this approach is the conviction (one he maintains can be demonstrated historically) that doctrinal beliefs are not the product of abstract thinking or metaphysical speculation, but are key points within an ongoing process of attempting to account satisfactorily for human experience – specifically, experience engendered by Jesus of Nazareth.

3.4 Interdisciplinary Insights

This conviction that the truthfulness of religious beliefs resides in their capacity to offer a satisfactory account of human experience, including its relationality, supplies a promising route for being able to claim anything about God beyond that experience. To help us progress further, we will broaden our exploration to embrace insights gleaned from phenomenological approaches to religion. In *The Sense of God*, English polymath John Bowker employs the findings of their putative founder, Edmund Husserl (1859–1938), to demonstrate that whilst there is no, to borrow his phrase, 'Phantom Bridge from experience to the conclusion of God',[76] the nature of religious experience can justifiably be considered to supply a springboard in God's direction (my analogy).

Starting with Husserl's notion of intentionality, its directional quality consisting of 'the movement from the subject which constitutes the object, and the movement from the *apparent* object which constitute the subject', he observes how consciousness is essentially (*epoché*) relational, manifesting most fundamentally as *alter ego* and then as intersubjectivity, consciousness of other consciousnesses, creating the appearance of a shared world:

> Here at once one sees the way through the apparent dilemma: provided one
> starts, not from solipsism as a primary philosophical puzzle but from *epoché*,

---

[76] John Bowker, *The Sense of God*, xvi, from the preface to the second edition. It is an image borrowed by Bowker from P. F. Schmidt (*Religious Knowledge*, 1961); see Bowker's *The Religious Imagination and the Sense of God* (Oxford: Oxford University Press, 1978), 240.

bracketing off all else but the givenness of consciousness, it becomes clear that among the constituents of consciousness (that which comes into appearance) is the manifestation of the *alter ego*. This has the same initial phenomenological status as other constituents of consciousness: 'In the ego, the *alter ego* manifests and confirms itself as an experienced presentation ... I experience the world not as my own private world but as an intersubjective world, one that is given to all human beings and which contains objects accessible to all'. (175, quoting Husserl)

What lends further support to the existence of an intersubjective world beyond consciousness is what Husserl describes as 'the consistency of their indices' – the observation that other consciousnesses appear to experience phenomena in similar ways. It should be noted that this apparent escape from idealism, or even solipsism, characterizes all human endeavour and is not restricted to the religious sphere. For example, an essential test in many scientific disciplines is reproducibility – the capacity for different experimenters to replicate results whether in the culturing of a new antibiotic, the manufacturing of graphene or the isolation of the cosmic (microwave) background radiation. Where this is possible, the resulting consistency supplies grounds for projecting beyond imagination and conscious experience to infer a reality which is, in some sense, other – suggesting that whilst such a 'reality' is only accessible through human consciousness and experience, it cannot necessarily be reduced to them. Bowker wonders whether this approach can be applied to the experience of God.

> But the question which was never adequately faced by Husserl is whether those appearances in consciousness are simply *giving rise* to the sense of God, or whether they are the sense of *God*. So far as the positive sciences are concerned, phenomenological reduction opens the way to a returning of reality to the world, not as a contribution to the debate about solipsism but because, no matter which way that debate is solved, the intersubjectivity and cross-indexing of appearances enable scientific procedures, and return that degree of necessary reality to the world. But in that case, what of the appearances of *God* in consciousness? If one examines these and finds that there are 'essential structures of these experiences' which enable intersubjectivity and cross-indexing, must one not examine the possibility that a comparable kind of reality must be returned to God, as was returned to the world, not as a contribution to scholastic debates or metaphysical arguments but as a fact demanded by particular modes of consciousness itself? (177, quoting Husserl, italics original)

In other publications, Bowker explains how religions can be thought of as products of what he describes as 'somatic exploration and exegesis' in which embodied consciousnesses seek to explore 'what exactly is it that this body is capable of doing, of experiencing, of being, of becoming?' and to offer a coherent account for what is discovered.[77] Within this process, 'conducive properties' call forth a response from us, seeking interpretation. He cites aesthetics as a case in point where a masterpiece communicates a sense of beauty and where, although observers may differ in their impressions, all acknowledge to being affected in a comparable way.[78] According to Bowker, responses to certain conducive properties such as beauty, goodness and truth evolved into religions whose very existence is evidence of the commonality of such experiences, of the consistency in the means by which they can be engendered and of the adequacy of the accounts offered for them. Quite simply, if the word 'God' did not resonate with a common pool of human experience, it could never have become a source of cohesion and community formation. What is more, guiding this evolution have been 'constraints' which shape and limit how God is conceived which are, in turn, correlated with human experience: belief that God is holy emerges from numinous experiences of awe and wonder, and so forth.[79] Further, whilst the resulting attempts to account for these conducive properties may be inadequate and provisional, they nonetheless bear witness to a transcendent Otherness that is enduring and beyond human invention: 'What we say is always corrigible and incomplete. But the conducive properties that invade the particular architecture of energy that humans happen to be point to a truth beyond themselves that is not incomplete, the truth to which we give the name of God'.[80]

It appears that ten years after endorsing his judgement concerning the impossibility of crossing the so-named 'Phantom Bridge from experience to the conclusion of God',[81] Bowker has identified a reliable conduit. Despite the objectifying inclinations implicit within his analogy (i.e. God as a destination to be reached), its underlying conviction resonates with our findings to date, namely that God is encountered experientially through participating in

---

[77] John Bowker, *Is God a Virus?*, 152; also *The Sacred Neuron: Extraordinary New Discoveries Linking Science and Religion* (New York: Taurus, 2005).

[78] 'Conducive properties are so called because (from the underlying Latin, *duco*, I lead) they lead from the perceived object to one set of events within us rather than another, and they do this with a highly stable consistency . . . .. So, while it is true that there is no single property of beauty that all must see, there are nevertheless many stable conducive properties that do lie in the objects or the people around us, and which evoke the judgements of satisfaction and value, and the vocabularies of beauty and goodness . . . .. This is the truly important conjunction in art, between skill and its competence to bring into being the conducive properties that evoke in the observer the emotion and the judgement of beauty or of other satisfaction'. Bowker, *Sacred Neuron*, 44, 50–1.

[79] On the cohesiveness of religions and the role of constraints, see Bowker, *Is God a Virus?*, 96–107, 151–67.

[80] Bowker, *Sacred Neuron*, 148.

[81] Cf. the preface to the new edition of *Sense of God* (1995) which reiterates his conclusions reached in *Religious Imagination* (1978), which he appears to revise in *Sacred Neuron* (2005).

a belief system, informed by supportive beliefs, which clothe our inchoate, pioneering faith – giving expression to our deepest thoughts and longings, interpreting our memories and experience, informing our conduct and hope, and relating us not only to the otherness of ourselves and other persons, but also to the transcendent Other in whom, to quote the Christian Scriptures, 'we live and move and have our being' (Acts 17:28). Put simply, believing is learning to live 'as if' God *is* in the fullest sense outlined earlier, thereby engendering the existential orientation within which God enters human consciousness – not as a construct or derivation, but as the 'thou' summoning forth our personhood, animating our being-in-relation.

Interestingly, support for this approach can be found in recent advances within neuroscience and, in particular, on the function of and relationship between the two cerebral hemispheres in the constituting of the self and its relation to the world beyond consciousness. In his much-acclaimed *The Master and His Emissary: The Divided Brain and the Making of the Western World*, psychiatrist Iain McGilchrist applies some of these findings to the role of belief in general and religious belief in particular. We conclude this section with an extended excerpt:

> Believing is not to be reduced to thinking that such-and-such might be the case. It is not a weaker form of thinking, laced with doubt. Sometimes we speak like this: 'I believe that the train leaves at 6.13', where 'I believe that' simply means that 'I think (but am not certain) that'. Since the left hemisphere is concerned with what is certain, with knowledge of the facts, its version of belief is that it is just absence of certainty. If the facts were certain, according to its view, you should be able to say 'I know that' instead. This view of belief comes from the left hemisphere's disposition towards the world: interest in what is useful, therefore fixed and certain (the train timetable is no good if you can't rely on it). So belief is just a feeble form of knowing, as far as it is concerned.
>
> But to believe in terms of the right hemisphere is different, because its disposition towards the world is different. The right hemisphere does not 'know' anything, in the sense of certain knowledge. For it, belief is a matter of care: it describes a relationship, where there is a calling and an answering, the root concept is 'responsibility'. Thus if I say that 'I believe in you', it does not mean that I think that such-and-such things are the case about you, but can't be certain that I am right. It means that I stand in a certain sort of relation of care towards you, that entails me in certain kinds of ways of behaving (acting and being) towards you, and entails on you the responsibility of certain ways of acting and being as well. It is an acting 'as if' certain things were true about you that in the nature of things *cannot* be certain. It has the characteristic right-hemisphere qualities of being a betweenness: a reverberative, 're-sonant', 'respons-ible' relationship, in which each party is altered by the other and by the relationship between the two, whereas the relationship of the

believer to the believed in the left-hemisphere sense is inert, unidirectional, and centres on control rather than care . . . .

This helps illuminate belief in God. This is not reducible to a question of a factual answer to the question 'does God exist?', assuming for the moment that the expression 'a factual answer' has a meaning. It is having an attitude, holding a disposition towards the world, whereby that world, as it comes into being for me, is one in which God belongs. The belief alters the world, but also alters me. Is it true that God exists? Truth is a disposition, one of being true to someone or something. One cannot believe in nothing and thus avoid belief altogether, simply because one cannot have *no* disposition towards the world, that being is itself a disposition. Some people choose to believe in materialism; they act 'as if' such a philosophy were true. An answer to the question whether God exists could only come from my acting 'as if' God is, and in this way being true to God, and experiencing God (or not, as the case may be) as true to me. If I am a believer, I have to believe in God, and God, if he exists, has to believe in me. Rather like Escher's hands, the belief must arise reciprocally, not by a linear process of reasoning. This acting 'as if' is not a sort of cop-out, an admission that 'really' one does not believe what one pretends to believe. Quite the opposite: as Hans Vaihinger understood, all *knowledge*, particularly scientific knowledge, is no more than an acting 'as if' certain models were, for the time being, true. Truth and belief, once more, as in their etymology, are profoundly connected. It is only the left hemisphere that thinks there is certainty to be found anywhere.[82]

4 Monotheistic Belief

4.1 Clarifications

Having discussed in general terms four possible dimensions to religious belief, in this section we move on to explore monotheistic belief in particular from expressive, interpretative, formative and referential perspectives. Before doing so, however, we need to offer a number of clarifications. First, in recognition of McGrath's emphasis on the impossibility of adopting an objective stance, unmediated by human subjectivity or interpretative tradition, together with the understanding of faith developed in Section 2, we propose to rename the fourth dimension of belief as *relational* rather than referential. Hopefully, this more adequately reflects the personal contribution within truth claims about who or what is believed in, whilst emphasizing that we are relationally constituted integrities for whom relating to the beyond-self, to the other, is constitutive, not simply derivative, of our human being. It follows from this that if such relating is illusory, we would need to redraw the contours of our anthropology, which in turn brings into focus the constraining affects of our understanding of

---

[82] McGilchrist, *Master and His Emissary*, 170–1, italics original.

selfhood upon faith and belief. For example, where the self is essentially defined prior to any attempt to engage with the world beyond cognitive experience (cf. *cogito ergo sum*), then truth claims purporting to be about the transcendent are necessarily dependent upon, rather that integral to, our sense of self. By contrast, if selfhood is rooted in being-in-relation, of an existential orientation towards transcendence, then the quest for the other is as much about personal integrity as it is about the possibility of encounter.

Second, it should also be noted that the word 'monotheism' is, in certain respects, tautologous. The American philosopher and theologian David Bentley Hart, during an exposition of Christian belief, comments that 'the very division between monotheism and polytheism is in many cases a confusion of categories', before proposing that, whilst most of the major global religious traditions accommodate divine figures, 'gods', of one form or another, they equally bear witness to a single originating and sustaining source of all that is, to God. His distillation of their teaching in this respect is both apposite and succinct.

> To speak of 'God' properly, then – to use the word in a sense consonant with the teachings of orthodox Judaism, Christianity, Islam, Sikhism, Hinduism, Bahá'í, a great deal of antique paganism, and so forth – is to speak of the one infinite source of all that is: eternal, omniscient, omnipotent, omnipresent, uncreated, uncaused, perfectly transcendent of all things and for that very reason absolutely imminent to all things. God so understood is not something posed over and against the universe, in addition to it, nor is he the universe in itself. He is not a 'being', at least not in the way that a tree, a shoemaker, or a god is a being; he is not one more object in the inventory of things that are, or any sort of discrete object at all. Rather, all things that exist receive their being continuously from him, who is the infinite wellspring of all that is, *in whom* (to use the language of the Christian Scriptures) all things live and move and have their being. In one sense he is 'beyond being', if by 'being' one means the totality of discrete, finite things. In another sense he is 'being itself', in that he is the inexhaustible source of all reality, the absolute upon which the contingent is always utterly dependent, the unity and simplicity that underlies and sustains the diversity of finite and composite things. Infinite being, infinite consciousness, infinite bliss, from whom we are, by whom we know and are known, and in whom we find our only true consummation. All the great theistic traditions agree that God, understood in this proper sense, is essentially beyond finite comprehension; hence, much of the language used of him is negative in form and has been reached only by a logical process of abstraction from those qualities of finite reality that make it insufficient to account for its own existence. All agree as well, however, that he can genuinely be known; that is, reasoned toward, intimately encountered, directly experienced with a fullness surpassing mere conceptual comprehension.[83]

---

[83] Hart, *Experience of God*, 30–1.

Putting to one side his unfortunate use of gendered language for the divine, Hart strongly advocates that any satisfactory definition of the word 'God' which is informed by most, if not all, of the principal religious belief systems of the world, denotes exclusivity, thereby rendering further qualification, *mono*theism, redundant. In fact, such qualification risks causing confusion by eroding the boundary between divine beings, *daimonia*, and the one essential God. Further, monotheism is potentially misleading because it gives the impression that numerical categories – mono, poly – are meaningful in relation to God; that oneness is an appropriate characteristic of divine being. Again, this can be unhelpful, although it does depend on how the word is being used. For example, in Section 1, we introduced the distinction between confessional and metaphysical monotheism – the former denoting exclusive commitment to a particular deity, without prejudging whether other deities exist, constituting a *disposition* adopted by believers, with the latter denoting a value judgement about deity per se in the form of a *proposition* purporting to communicate information about divine essence. If Hart is on the right lines, then metaphysical monotheism should omit the 'mono' because God, properly conceived, is unique; in the case of confessional monotheism, however, 'mono' qualifies a believer's allegiance, stressing its exclusiveness, and is significant, resonating with the first commandment of the Jewish Decalogue: 'I am the LORD your God, who brought you out of the land of Egypt, out of the house of slavery; you shall have no other gods before me' (Exodus 20:2–3).

Third, we should keep in mind the implications of our discussion of monotheistic belief for religious pluralism or, to borrow Lindbeck's term, for ecumenism. In Section 3, we noted how he concluded that ecumenical considerations (cf. the 'possibility of doctrinal reconciliation without capitulation') called into question referential truth claims about God. This, we observed, has been challenged by Alister McGrath, amongst others, who criticizes him for conceptualizing doctrinal truth in abstraction, giving insufficient acknowledgement to the role of interpretative traditions and their communities within doctrinal formulation. Although McGrath's approach is foundationally Christological and, as such, does not readily serve as an 'ecumenical' paradigm, his criticism does draw attention to an important distinction and one that informs much pluralist and some inclusivist approaches, namely between the *explanandum* and the *explanans*; that is to say, between God, the source of all human experience of transcendence, and human attempts to account for that experience and be enlightened by it, which through time and cultural appropriation crystallize into thoroughgoing belief systems, into religions. Whilst the latter, as we noted in Section 2, may supply the environment and hermeneutical index for encountering the former, it cannot be equated with it for one of two reasons.

Firstly, although expressive, interpretative and formative approaches to belief attempt to explain the phenomenon of God exclusively in human terms, whereby our *explanans* becomes the *explanandum*, we are in the process of assembling grounds for concluding that it is in fact our self-understanding as relational beings who realize their personhood through encountering the non-self, the other, together with the recognition that certain readily accessible and repeatable human responses both engender and constrain interpretations in terms of transcendence, which opens up the possibility of God being that Other, the prevenient progenitor, who, in a profound sense, is the fulfilment of our human vocation. And yet, secondly, without in any way wishing to contradict this, it must also be acknowledged that even if belief systems cannot be accounted for exclusively in terms of human ingenuity, they are nonetheless subject to the vicissitudes of human endeavour, rendering any religion ultimately partial, approximate, provisional and corrigible, whilst paradoxically possessing the capacity to offer a convincing and satisfying vehicle for faith. As a consequence, it is conceivable that each religion represents a different encultured embodiment of faith and attempts to account for its discoveries.

A partial analogy is supplied by human beings falling in love, participating in ecstatic transcendence in relation to another person, where both parties experience an expansiveness in their own selfhood engendered by one whose unfathomable otherness, incapable of being reduced to each's expectations of a 'perfect partner', is paradoxically the source of a mutual sense of fulfilment. Manifestly, we do not all fall in love with the same person, but through the particularity of our own relationship we gain access not only to a common pool of human experience, but also to encountering the otherness of being which is both embodied and yet transcends embodiment, relating us essentially to love's source – a mystery celebrated in that most erotic and theological biblical composition, the Song of Solomon: 'Awake, O north wind, and come, O south wind! Blow upon my garden that its fragrance may be wafted abroad. Let my beloved come to his garden, and eat its choicest fruits' (4:16). With these comments in mind, we turn to our examination of the four dimensions of monotheistic belief.

4.2 Expressive Belief

One of the seminal insights that both John Bowker and Iain McGilchrist underlined in the previous section is that we experience the outside world not as *cogito*, detached minds discrete from and independent of whatever may be beyond the thinking self, but as *embodied consciousnesses* whose being is located within space and time, woven within a web of interrelatedness. As such, we do not possess a body like we possess a coat or a pair of shoes with which to clothe the naked self; rather, we are somatic entities who relate principally through our senses.[84] At least one important corollary follows from this, namely that we are practitioners before we are theorists – embodiment is our principal modus operandi. We don't make sense of the world, finding meaning in abstraction from any social imaginary, and then decide which one to subscribe to and, as a consequence, how best to invest our time and energy; rather, it is through relating to and actively engaging in a particular belief system that meaning emerges. This is because we are situated, contextualized beings whose entire experience is mediated and, as a consequence, meaning is embedded within the imaginary we inhabit and embrace through participation. Further, although participation is a personal choice, it tends to conform to certain communally recognized practices which are, owing to their strategic role within that system, inherently meaningful.[85] For instance, undertaking empirical research within the scientific community is meaningful principally because it is how you participate in that community and only secondarily because of any significance an individual researcher may choose to invest in it.[86] Or again, wearing a uniform is meaningful because of its role within the organization to which a person belongs rather than because of personal preference. The philosopher, Mark Johnson, summarizes the implications of this embodied approach thus:

> We humans live in a human-related world, for even the more-than-human world can only be understood and engaged by us via the structures and processes of human understanding and action. All meaning is human meaning – meaning grounded in our human bodies, in their humanly encountered environments. All of the meaning we can make and all of the values we hold grow out of our humanity-interacting-with-our-world.
>
> Our humanity encompasses our animal needs, our personal relationships, our need and capacity for love, our social relations, our cultural institutions and practices, and our spirituality. We make sense of all of these dimensions

---

[84] See, for example, Maurice Merleau-Ponty's classic, *Phenomenology of Perception*, trans. Donald A. Landes (London: Routledge, 2012 [French original, 1945]); also Mark Johnson's *The Meaning of the Body: Aesthetics of Human Understanding* (Chicago: University of Chicago Press, 2007).

[85] Especially, the work of Pierre Bourdieu on his understanding of practical reason and the role of the habitus in *The Logic of Practice*, trans. Richard Nice (Stanford, CA: Stanford University Press, 1990), 52 and *Outline of a Theory of Practice*.

[86] Cf. 'The study of paradigms ... is what mainly prepares the student for membership in the particular scientific community with which he will later practice. Because he there joins men who learned the bases of their field from the same concrete models, his subsequent practice will seldom evoke overt disagreement over fundamentals. Men whose research is based on shared paradigms are committed to the same rules and standards for scientific practice. That commitment and the apparent consensus it produces are prerequisites for normal science, i.e., for the genesis and continuation of any particular research tradition'. Kuhn, *Scientific Revolutions*, 10–11.

of our being by means of body-based feeling, conceptualization, reasoning, and symbolic expressions. Our aspirations for transcendence must be realised not in attempts to escape our bodily habitation, but rather by employing it in our ongoing efforts to transform ourselves and our world for the better.[87]

James Smith, another philosopher, this time with theological proclivities, draws heavily on Merleau-Ponty, as well as Bourdieu, Johnson and others, to adumbrate what he describes as a liturgical anthropology. In his *Cultural Liturgies* trilogy,[88] Smith develops the thesis that humans are *homo liturgicus*, inherently worshipping animals who pursue their desires and who 'inhabit the world not primarily as thinkers, or even believers, but as more affective, embodied creatures who make [their] way in the world more by feeling [their] way around it' (1.47). As a consequence, we are formed by what we love ultimately, 'which constitutes an affective, gut-like orientation to the world that is prior to reflection and even eludes conceptual articulation' (1.51). What distinguishes humans, therefore, is 'not *whether* we love, but *what* we love' (1.52, italics original). Although Smith's overall project is to develop a paradigm for Christian education as liturgical formation – and we shall return to him when exploring the formational dimension of monotheistic belief – here we wish to focus on his readily acknowledged Augustinian insight, namely that human beings are inherently desiring creatures. This resonates with the relational ontology developed earlier, but by elevating the significance of a particular species of relating, he is able to demonstrate that worship is constitutive of human being. As part of this, he stresses both its intentional and teleological nature whilst, given its pre- or non-cognitive quality, focusing on the processes of habituation which characterize love's aim and love's end:

> We have now articulated an alternative to the person-as-thinker and person-as
> -believer models in the person-as-lover model. We have highlighted four key
> elements in this model: Human persons as intentional creatures whose fun-
> damental way of 'intending' the world is love or desire. This love or desire –
> which is unconscious or noncognitive – is always aimed at some vision of the
> good life, some particular articulation of the kingdom. What primes us to be
> so oriented – and act accordingly – is a set of habits or dispositions that are
> formed in us through affective, bodily means, especially bodily practices,

---

[87] Johnson, *Meaning of the Body*, 282–3.

[88] *Desiring the Kingdom: Worship, Worldview, and Cultural Formation*, Cultural Liturgies Volume 1 (Grand Rapids, MI: Baker Academic, 2009); *Imagining the Kingdom: How Worship Works*, Cultural Liturgies Volume 2 (Grand Rapids, MI: Baker Academic, 2013); *Awaiting the King: Reforming Public Theology*, Cultural Liturgies Volume 3 (Grand Rapids, MI: Baker Academic, 2017).

routines, or rituals that grab hold of our hearts through our imagination, which is closely linked to our bodily senses.[89]

If Smith is on the right lines, then, first and foremost, monotheistic belief affirms that human beings are inherently worshipping creatures because they are constituted relationally, finding fulfilment and integrity within a particular species of relating characterized by love. But more than that, monotheistic belief informs a belief system within which this essential human desire can be channelled in ways that are both commensurate with the personal investment that devotion entails and consummatory in the sense of supplying a means of fulfilment. Monotheism orientates the worshipper to a source, to a transcendent Other, who is worthy of our worship. What is more, it affirms that if human desiring is to escape the dangers of Narcissus and Baal, of self-infatuation and idolatry, it must necessarily be exclusive in its focus and wholehearted in its execution. From an expressive perspective, this insight clarifies the nature of love's vocation. Just as there are, in theory, any number of persons one could marry, once the knot has been tied, there can be only one if the expansiveness of human being characterizing love's vocation is to be experienced satisfactorily, so worship is necessarily singular in its attention and thoroughgoing in its intention – as Augustine's oft-repeated confession affirms: 'You inspire us to take delight in praising you, for you have made us for yourself, and our hearts are restless until they rest in you' (*tu excitas ut laudare te delectet, quia fecisti nos ad te et inquietum est cor nostrum donec requiescat in te*).[90]

4.3 Interpretative Belief

As we noted in Section 2, most, if not all, religions as belief systems possess an internal coherence which is part of their plausibility, including an interpretative framework of beliefs enabling believers to experience being human in a particular way. In many cases, the explicatory function of these beliefs resides within the overall imaginary to which they belong, where they constitute a strand within a complex hermeneutical web of meaning. For instance, the Christian doctrine of the Incarnation offers an interpretation of the life, death and resurrection of Jesus of Nazareth, but its significance derives from a nexus of other beliefs relating to divine being, the human condition, the reality of sin and so forth. As such, its elucidatory capacity resides within that nexus and largely evaporates outside of it: the Incarnation doesn't make much sense unless one believes in an interventionist God of love, in one's own captivity to the

---

[89] Smith, *Desiring the Kingdom*, 62–3.   [90] Augustine, *Confessions* 1.1 (LCL 26).

thrall of sin and in the salvific efficacy of the atonement.[91] For this reason, although many believers in the Incarnation believe with universal intent – believing that, although it emerged within the Christian imaginary, it belongs to the human race – it remains largely meaningless, lacking explicatory force, outside of that sponsoring tradition. There are some beliefs, however, that attempt to account for phenomena that are universally acknowledged, irrespective of belief system. One of the most obvious and compelling examples was framed by the German philosopher, Gottfried Wilhelm Leibniz (1646–1716), in his now famous dictum: 'Why is there something rather than nothing?'[92]

A scholar who in recent years has brought considerable clarity to where the interpretative capacity of monotheistic belief resides in relation to this fundamental question is David Bentley Hart. Starting with the experience of wonder, the 'ontological surprise' of the sheer gratuitousness of being, he points out that

> ... nothing within experience has any 'right' to be, any power to give itself existence .... The world is unable to provide any account of its own actuality .... Nothing within the cosmos contains the ground of its own being .... Simply said, one is contingent through and through, partaking of being rather than generating it out of some source within oneself; and the same is true of the whole intricate web of interdependencies that constitutes nature. (88–9, 92–3)

From this recognition, he argues that the origin of the contingent universe is not a problem that, given sufficient time, scientists will be able to solve because nonexistence is not *quantitatively* different from existence, a condition within the dependent order such as black holes or dark energy, but *qualitatively* different: 'It is a difference that no merely quantitative calculation of processes or forces or laws can ever overcome. Physical reality cannot account for its own existence for the simple reason that nature – the physical – is that which by definition already exists; existence ... lies logically beyond the system of causes that nature comprises; it is, quite literally, "hyperphysical," or, shifting into Latin, *super naturam*' (95–6).

Hart employs the principle of causality (cf. 'all things that do not possess the cause of their existence in themselves must be brought into existence by something outside themselves ... the contingent is always contingent on something else' [99]) to demonstrate that whilst the current manifestation of the contingent universe may have arisen from a previous or, in some sense, concurrent manifestation, at the source of any chain of causality, as Aristotle

---

[91] It could also be argued that, in addition to these attendant theological beliefs, the Incarnation is dependent upon philosophical beliefs, such as Middle Platonism.

[92] Gottfried Wilhelm Leibniz, 'Principles of Nature and Grace Based on Reason' (1714), 7; trans. Jonathan Bennett, 2017; accessed via www.earlymoderntexts.com/assets/pdfs/leibniz1714a.pdf.

recognized centuries earlier, cannot be another cause that does not possess in itself the grounds of its own being; rather, there must, logically and metaphysically, 'be some truly *unconditioned* reality (which, by definition, cannot be temporal or spatial or in any sense finite) upon which all else depends; otherwise nothing could exist at all. And it is this unconditioned and eternally sustaining source of being that classical metaphysics, East and West, identifies as God' (106). In a memorable passage, Hart offers further clarification of the God who the very 'thatness' of the contingent universe seems to demand in order to account for its existence:

> As Thomas Aquinas rightly points out, therefore, creation from nothingness cannot be some event that occurs at a given moment within time. Neither can it constitute a transition from one state of reality to another, since nothingness is not some kind of substance in which a change can take place. It is wholly an act of prime or essential causation, the eternal gift of *esse* ... to a reality that has no ground of being in itself. And God, therefore, is the creator of all things not as the first temporal agent in cosmic history (which would make him not the prime cause of creation but only the initial secondary cause within it), but as the eternal reality in which 'all things live, and move, and have their being', present in all things as the actuality of all actualities, transcendent of all things as the changeless source from which all actuality flows. It is only when one properly understands this distinction that one can also understand what the contingency of created things might tell us about who or what God is.[93]

Next, Hart turns to why such a God must be infinite actuality incorporating 'absolute being, omniscience, omnipotence, perfect beatitude, and so forth' as pure white light 'contains the full visible spectrum in its simple unity' (132). Furthermore, God 'cannot be composed of and so dependent upon severable constituents, physical or metaphysical, as then he would himself be conditional .... The infinite power of being – the power to be, without any reliance upon some other cause of being, as well as the power to impart being to creatures – must be of infinite capacity, which means infinite simplicity' (134–5). At this stage in the argument, Hart leaves open the question of divine motivation, although he maintains this has little impact upon his case, which is essentially an inescapable deduction of reason: '*Why* the Absolute produces the contingent may be inconceivable for us; but *that* the contingent can exist only derivatively, receiving its existence from the absolute, is a simple deduction of reason. Alternatively, reality is essentially absurd: absolute contingency, unconditional conditionality, and uncaused effect. And the antithesis between the two positions can never be made any less stark than that' (147, italics original).

---

[93] Hart, *Experience of God*, 106–7.

Whilst Hart's thesis is more nuanced than space allows us to explore here, hopefully by incorporating a sample of his prose, we have managed to communicate something of both the logical and rhetorical force of his case. There may well be questions about divine motivation, as well as about the 'mechanism' by which infinite actuality donates being, but what seems incontrovertible is that Hart brings fresh intellectual rigour to causality's seemingly inescapable conclusion with respect to the existence of the contingent order, and one that is entirely congruent with monotheistic belief.

4.4 Formative Belief

In Section 3, we discussed George Lindbeck's cultural-linguistic paradigm where doctrinal beliefs serve as 'communally authoritative rules of discourse, attitude, and action' which, along with a religious tradition's 'cosmic stories or myths, and ethical directives are integrally related to the rituals it practices, the sentiments or experiences it evokes, the actions it recommends, and the institutional forms it develops'.[94] Whether or not one is persuaded by his overall programme, Lindbeck convincingly highlights not only the formational dimension of belief, but also the embeddedness of belief within the habitus characterizing a believing community. As we have seen, both of these inform James Smith's liturgical anthropology and pedagogy of embodiment, where human beings as affective desirers inhabit, in his case, a Christian imaginary which, through participation, forms a Christocentric-kingdom orientation within worshippers whilst inculcating a Christoform pattern of living. Again, one does not need to subscribe unequivocally to Smith's project to recognize that believing constitutes an embodied response in which the dispositional components – the habitus: rituals, practices and so forth – exert a formative influence through channelling human desire and relating us aright, as well as supplying existential content or phronesis to beliefs.

As a way into how these insights might bear upon the formative dimension of monotheistic belief, let us consider a comparable phenomenon – monogamy, the state or practice of being married to a single spouse. At one level, it is possible to engage with this intellectually without recourse to experience or personal investment, where belief might affirm that there is nothing logically incoherent about this estate, or it might constitute assent that monogamy is actually practised among the human race, or it might even express the conviction that one considers it a desirable condition in which to partake. In each of these cases, monogamy is being objectified and evaluated dispassionately, according to the prevailing rationality, although the last case entertains the

---

[94] Lindbeck, *Nature of Doctrine*, 18, 33.

prospect of subjective engagement. However, at another level, there is an altogether different way of believing in monogamy, one that erupts from the passion of sexual attraction and embodied desire for another person. A thoroughgoing human response, engaging the heart as much, if not more, than the head – one that, for all its particularity, is shaped by cultural norms which unconsciously inform expectations and channel desires, steering the couple through the liminality of engagement or betrothal to making uncondi-tional commitments to one another, ritualized in a marriage ceremony, as each party is initiated into a new identity within the community, embodied within culturally determined practices (e.g. cohabitation, sexual intimacy, parenthood) and disciplines (e.g. fidelity, cooperation, worth-ship) in which, through mutual support, practice and conforming pressures, they gradually become proficient and habituated. These are practices and disciplines that are not arbitrary, optional or tangential, as if it were possible to experience monogamy without them; rather, they constitute the integral habits, the distillations of a culture's practical wisdom (phronesis), which supply both the generative core of monog-amous living and its constraints to the extent that, whilst the prospect of polygamy may be logically or practically conceivable, even in certain respects desirable, at the level of lived experience, it is a contradiction in terms because it corresponds to a different species of relationship.[95] That is to say, the fruits of experimentation through time have yielded the insight that there is something within the dynamics of fidelity, unconditionality and total acceptance that possesses the potential for mediating an intimacy of relating and expansiveness of personhood not accessible through other configurations. And, again, although believing in monogamy in this embodied sense can be challenged,[96] it has stood the test of time during which it has emerged within or been adopted by many different cultures, religions and ideologies around the world. It should also be pointed out that if there is any practical wisdom enshrined in *arranged marriages* with reference to our discussion, then it would appear to run along the lines that, whilst the practices and disciplines characterizing monogamy can both channel and give expression to passionate desire, they also possess the

---

[95] See Smith's discussion of 'thin' ('mundane') and 'thick' ('meaning-full') practices/habits in *Desiring the Kingdom*, 80–5.

[96] For example, polygamy is both legal and practised in many countries throughout Africa and Asia. However, this is not incompatible with the belief, held at whatever level, that monogamy constitutes a different species of relationship. Equally, neither are high levels of divorce where citizens are only permitted one spouse – not least, because, in many cases and for whatever reason, the cause of breakdown is an unwillingness or incapacity to become habituated in the practices and disciplines characterizing monogamy. Further, monogamy has been interrogated from a feminist perspective, for example Germaine Greer, *The Female Eunuch* (London: Flamingo, 1993; orig. 1970) and Kate Millett, *Sexual Politics* (New York: Doubleday, 1970).

capacity in certain circumstances to engender such desire, suggesting a complex relation between form and content, practice and experience, shape and spirit.

What then of monotheistic belief? At one level, it expresses the conviction about whether God *is* and, if so, about the essential nature of God. It could also be an affirmation about the worthiness of God, even of a person's willingness to contemplate what believing in such a God might entail. However, as with monogamy, the formational potential of monotheistic belief resides at an existential level where it supplies the cornerstone of a religious imaginary within which our inchoate faith, that trusting openness to the otherness of being and the being of others, can not only be owned and expressed, but also explored through being orientated towards and related to that transcendent Other who is faith's ultimate vocation. Monotheistic belief, therefore, is the backbone of an all-encompassing sacred anatomy animating the lived experience of host communities and their members. This is nowhere more in evidence than in corporate worship, which to the outsider may appear to be a waste of time – adding nothing to material survival or betterment, or even to furthering the humanitarian goals forming an essential component of any belief system. But this is precisely the point: the act of making space in a busy routine, putting to one side the distractions and demands of day-to-day living, in order to focus on one whose 'being' is entirely gratuitous and whose gratuitous donation of being sustains all being, is the epitome of monotheism. Further, each liturgy invites worshippers to participate in what can be described as *sacred play* as they inhabit a new identity as faith-filled believers finding their place within a covenant of belonging born of grace and discover their true vocation as disciples of the one true God. Along the way, through the offering of praise and thanksgiving, attending to Scripture and its exposition, affirming and embracing foundational beliefs, interceding for the needy, confessing failure and resolving to improve – by means of language, ritual, posture and often imagery and sacrament – the values, commitments, aspirations and patterns of behaviour of worshippers are gradually aligned with those of the sponsoring belief system. Although there is clearly an intentional component to this, as Smith and others have demonstrated, much of the formational effect of monotheistic belief, like any core belief, is unconscious and pre-cognitive, integrated within the entire belief system, from the architecture and arrangement of worship space, through liturgies and observances, festivals and holy days, to rules of life and rites of passage.[97] All of this and more, reflecting the wisdom accrued through centuries, inclines *homo liturgicus* towards *homo monotheist*

---

[97] Especially, Smith, *Imagining the Kingdom*, 103–50 and David F. Ford, *Self and Salvation: Being Transformed* (Cambridge: Cambridge University Press, 1999).

as worshippers undergo a relativizing of worth within their lives in which potential idols are relegated to a significance commensurate with their inherent capacity for wholesome human flourishing (so prescribed) and compatible with allegiance to the one in whom 'we live and move and have our being'. Put simply, in terms of formational belief, monotheism is more of a verb than a noun, a process than a destination, giving rise to a belief system through which faith is encouraged and enabled to explore being-in-relation to the source of transcendence immanent in all things, whilst desire is inclined towards the worship of what is worthy and capable of sustaining our devotion.

4.5 Relational Belief

So far in this section, we have considered how monotheistic belief can possess an expressive, interpretative or formative dimension within the exploration of faith and its constitutive role within human being. In the case of the second, where the principle of causality seems to require a 'truly *unconditioned* reality ... upon which all else depends',[98] whilst this conclusion represents, at one level, no more than a construct of human thought, an attempt to make sense of the universe, it nonetheless appears to identify a necessary truth about an 'uncaused cause', albeit not one grounded in personal experience. This raises the much-debated question about whether beliefs can be true not only in the sense of their utility within our exploration of human being, but also in bearing witness to a transcendent Other who, in some sense, is beyond us. To help clarify what form such bearing witness might take, let us pause for a moment to consider the oft-cited ancient parable of the elephant and the blind men, where each of them touches a different part of the creature and claims that the mammal conforms to the limits of his tactile investigations. Afterwards, they are at loggerheads with one another, each claiming to possess the truth about the elephant, until an enlightened teacher explains that they are all both correct and in error – correct, in claiming to have encountered an elephant and to possess knowledge about the creature; in error, in not recognizing that their encounter was partial and could be expanded substantially by attending to the testimony of fellow witnesses.

What is helpful here is the implicit recognition that there is no access to the elephant, to God, apart from human experience and, as we have argued, our experience of God is shaped by the belief system or, in some cases, systems we inherited at birth or, at some juncture, into which we were subsequently assimilated.[99] One of the ways in which the parable is misleading, however, is

---

[98] Hart, *Experience of God*, 106.

[99] Although this insight is undermined, at least in part, by the teacher who somehow appears to have unmediated access to the entire creature. The parable of the elephant and blind men has many iterations throughout the ancient world, across different religions and philosophical schools.

that it objectifies God once more, conceiving the divine as a being among beings, one existing in space and time, open to empirical investigation. And it must be conceded here that the deployment of personal language – whether in referring to God as father, mother, king, judge and so forth, or to believers as God's children or disciples or whatever – can encourage this outlook: conceiving God to be, in some sense, a substantial person. Self-evidently, any attempt to speak of that which is beyond human experience and the productions of space-time is pushing language to its limits, hence the use of different forms of speech; but collapsing the analogical into the literal not only risks reducing God-talk to nonsense, but also missing a key insight which the appropriation of personal language communicates, namely that whilst God may not be a person, we relate to God personally, more like we relate to a person than to a thing – *ich and du*.

This brings us back to the monogamy analogy. At one level, it is self-evident that, unlike God, a spouse can be investigated empirically, generating an extensive register of metrics (e.g. weight, blood group, ethnicity, eye colour), characteristics (e.g. vegetarian, adventurous, musical, early riser) and medical history (e.g. caesarean birth, measles as a child, ovarian cancer, hysterectomy). However, this is information *about* someone in a comparable way that we could collect information about a pet dog or a specimen of a tree or pretty much anything, animate or inanimate. All of this would be readily verifiable and accessible to different investigators deploying similar equipment, techniques and methodology. Yet despite possessing this data, even if it included the results of mapping someone's genome, could one claim to know that person?

At one level, certainly, generating a biomedical and behavioural profile with significant predictive potential. And yet would not a spouse claim to encounter someone who transcends all these accidents of human being – a person only encounterable once the objectifying gaze has been averted and clamour for facts silenced, so that space can be found for those essential dynamics of personal relating and loving intimacy, where certainty gives way to trust, detachment to vulnerability, control to respect and evaluation to acceptance – a personal relating which doesn't seek to crack the code or fathom the depths, content to learn to live in a kind of communion with one who will always be out of reach, yet mysteriously immanent in the immediacy of bodily form and the plethora of interactions, exchanges and evolutions constituting covenant together? There can be no 'objective' proof of any of this. It may all be an epiphenomenon of physical processes and predictable behaviours without remainder; but, in a sense, that's beside the point, because these predictions belong to a different

---

A convenient summary of the narrative flow and usual moral conclusion is supplied by John Godfrey Saxe's (1816–87) poem, 'Blind Men and the Elephant'.

imaginary and one that is necessarily blind to love's truth. Yet there is evidence of a sort, for whilst the intercourses of love can be accounted for in terms of mundane actualities, for participants they seem to resist such reductive aetiologies, suggesting instead more expansive causalities emanating from the Otherness of being and the being of another – something the Welsh poet R. S. Thomas captures succinctly when he writes:

> There was a room
> apart she kept herself in,
> teasing me by leading me
> to its glass door, only
> to confront me with
> my reflection. I learned from her
> even so. Walking her shore
> I found things cast up
> from her depths that spoke
> to me of another order,
> worshipper as I was
> of untamed nature.[100]

Thomas composed 'Together' in honour of his first wife, Mildred Eldridge, known as Elsi, although, as with much of his work, it is no less revealing of his relationship with God. And whilst we cannot investigate God in a comparable manner to how we would set about investigating Elsi, or any person, there are nonetheless grounds for belief as David Bentley Hart has demonstrated; and then there are those 'castings along the shore' when faith engages us in the heuristics of personal encounter: donations of being constituting a contingent universe; sacrifices of love resourced from beyond; reserves of sustenance sufficient for the task; superfluities of vitality animating nature's fecundity; distillations of hope overwhelming despair; sacraments of grace transubstantiated within the quotidian; bestowals of forgiveness liberating the future from the past; intensities of suffering with power to atone; discoveries of wisdom beyond human invention; incarnations of beauty manifest within the productions of time.[101] All of these and more are evidenced within the stuff of life, and yet, when experienced within a monotheistic belief system, thereby gaining fresh intensity and significance, they become overtures of transcendent Otherness, beckoning us to commune.

---

[100] R. S. Thomas, 'Together', in *Residues* (Highgreen, Tarset: Bloodaxe Books, 2002), 27.
[101] See, for example, the discussion of aesthetics in Edward Robinson, *The Language of Mystery* (London: SCM, 1987) and George Steiner, *Real Presences: Is There Anything in What We Say?* (London: Faber & Faber, 1989).

There is truth here – *alêtheia*, uncovering – if one can venture beyond the reaches of what Charles Taylor describes as the 'buffered self'[102] conceived within a secular imaginary blinded to transcendence and, equally importantly, find one's place within an imaginary in which it becomes visible, accessible, relatable to – one that has exorcised the most beguiling form of idolatry, an unswerving and unjustifiable belief in the sufficiency of human progress to account for everything, including its own lack of self-sufficiency.[103]

5 Concluding Remarks

5.1 Summarizing Our Findings

Throughout Sections 2–4, we have been working towards a monotheistic phenomenology of belief. Adopting a relational ontology and starting with faith as an essential human characteristic, an ecstatic, individuating impulse orientating us towards transcendence, we have suggested that belief systems such as religions can serve as social imaginaries in which our existential openness to otherness can be explored, interpreted and fruitfully engaged. Within such imaginaries, beliefs, which can fulfil different functions (expressive, interpretative, formative and relational), supply an anatomy for faith, giving form and colour to the common life of the embodying community, as well as shape and content to the lived experience of participating believers. Further, we noted that beliefs are not theoretical abstractions from living, but heuristic distillations of faith's explorations and insights. As a consequence, believing extends well beyond intellectual assent to embrace all of life – a capacity acquired through time to perceive and experience human being through the prism of a belief system and to invest oneself accordingly through inhabiting that system's traditions, routines and commitments, as well as through imaginative improvisation and application.

Within this hermeneutical framework, we considered the various dimensions of monotheistic belief; for instance, from an expressive perspective, how it affirms and evokes our inherent capacity for worship and, as relationally constituted beings, both orientates and channels our desire – relating us to a source worthy of our devotion and capable of drawing us out of ourselves into a more expansive integrity when exercised within worship's most fruitful framework, covenantal love. Moving on and taking our lead from David Bentley Hart, we discovered that monotheistic belief still possesses considerable interpretative capacity when attempting to address some of the most

---

[102] In contrast to the 'porous self'; see Taylor, *Secular Age*, 37–43, et al.

[103] See Tony Eagleton's critique of liberal humanism in *Reason, Faith, and Revolution: Reflections on the God Debate* (New Haven, CT: Yale University Press, 2009).

fundamental and necessary existential questions, such as: why is there some-thing rather than nothing? From the recognition that nothing within the universe can fully account for its own actuality, we were persuaded by application of the principle of causation that the contingent order ultimately owes its existence to an 'unconditioned and eternally sustaining source of being' which is both beyond space-time and yet infuses every contingency – possessing infinite actuality and perfect simplicity: one that monotheistic belief systems acknow-ledge as God.

From a formational perspective, we noted how monotheistic belief supplies the backbone of an all-encompassing sacred anatomy animating the lived experience of host communities and their members. In particular, we explored how the different components and contexts of corporate worship, consciously and unconsciously, exert a formational effect on participants – inclining them towards a being-in-relation-to-God. Following on from this, we noted how such being-in-relation, usually mediated through a belief system,[104] brings into focus those 'castings along the shore', those gratuitous surpluses manifest within the stuff of existence, which resonate with faith's ecstatic vocation and mediate personal encounter with the transcendent One whose donation of being is the source and sustenance of all that is. We inquired: does this constitute proof of God? It depends on which imaginary you are inhabiting; but it does seem to be as close to a truth claim as personal relating affords and, within such relating, it is sufficient – in fact, it is essentially so. Consider for a moment how each person is ultimately a mysterious integrity, who is only knowable in relation and then only in part – yet still we claim to know and even to love and enter into covenant with them. Can we expect personal relating to deliver any more with respect to God? And what would 'more' mean in this context? Yet, in each case, living in each other's light, however opaque, yields its own amplitude.

In sum, then, monotheistic belief is an embodiment of human being, one that not only gives expression to faith's inclination towards self-transcendence, but also, through participating in a sponsoring belief system, relates the believer to faith's source of fulfilment through learning to live in God's light. It should be noted that such belief as adumbrated throughout this Element is intrinsically *panentheistic* in a manner that is entirely compatible with monotheism. In contrast to pantheism, where the divine is identified with some components

---

[104] This qualification needs to be made because of those claiming unmediated access to the divine through mystical experiences which often emerge within a particular belief system, yet subse-quently appear to 'shed' it. This is a vast and controversial area, but see Bernard McGinn's analysis in *The Foundations of Mysticism: Origins to the Fifth Century* (London: SCM, 1991), 265–343. Also the apophatic traditions or *via negativa* of, for example, Vedanta Hinduism, Jewish Kabbala, Eastern Christianity and Sufi Islam.

within or, indeed, with the entire material universe or, again, with forces of nature, panentheistic belief recognizes that divine being is immanent within the universe, whilst transcending it.[105] God is not identified with the universe, but infuses it, as vitality infuses living creatures or beauty a work of art. Similarly, and stretching analogical thinking further, just as a living creature doesn't possess a bit of vitality, nor is vitality thereby divided or diminished by animating many, so God is immanently present throughout the universe without division or dilution.

5.2 Anticipating Questions

In a very real sense, then, monotheism is a hypothesis only verifiable through personal experience. But does this not open it up to the charge of being no more than a fantasy – of living a delusion, as we touched on in Section 2? Potentially, but no more so than any other belief system, religious or secular, because, as we have seen, they all depend on presuppositions of one sort or another, gaining legitimation from premises beyond empirical verification. Yet whilst each system undoubtedly shapes attitudes, outlooks and expectations, the practice of living remains the ultimate arbiter for whether monotheistic belief rings true, resonating with experience and satisfying our hunger for self-transcendence, whilst enabling us to engage fruitfully with those fundamental existential challenges characterizing the human condition. Further, there is one more insight to reflect on which comes into focus when we consider whether there is any difference between 'being in love with being in love' and 'being in love with someone who is in love with you'. At times, they may appear identical; but the former, transcendentally vacuous, lacks any capacity to surprise or to bestow worth or to be present relationally in any meaningful sense. I wonder if a similar distinction can be drawn between 'believing in a God in whom we wish to believe' and 'believing in a God who transcends our beliefs'.

Anticipating another question, this time one likely to be raised by monotheistic believers: why hasn't special revelation been given greater consideration? After all, the divine origin of the Torah and Quran, along with the Incarnation of God's Word, are central beliefs within the three principal monotheistic religions. Regrettably, space does not permit a full response, so a number of preliminary observations must suffice. First, although special revelation appears to be of a different order from the general revelation of natural theology, it is in certain key respects similar – for example, they both represent attempts to supply satisfactory accounts for particular phenomena. Whether one is seeking

---

[105] Cf. John Macquarrie's dialectical concept of God in *In Search of Deity: An Essay in Dialectical Theism* (London: SCM, 1984), 171–84.

to account satisfactorily for why there is something rather than nothing or for the emergence of Scripture or for the enduring impact of Jesus of Nazareth, controversy does not tend to reside around the phenomena per se, but around their significance and ultimate provenance. In each case, the emphasis falls upon the word 'satisfactorily'.[106]

Second, special revelation and, in particular, belief that at certain junctures in space-time God relates to the universe in a modified way have significant implications for monotheistic belief. For one thing, they imply that God embraces change either in the sense of choosing to do something or responding to happenings in creation (which raises further problems).[107] For another and related matter, they seem to suggest that there is both spatiality and temporality within God – that God is not equally immanent at all times and places, but invests certain persons or moments with additional donations of divine being. But, again, is this compatible with monotheistic belief?

Third, given all human experience is mediated, special revelation seems to presuppose an existing belief system capable of recognizing a new happening and interpreting it accordingly.[108] It would appear, then, that special revelation implies, even requires, the receptivity of recognition that only an adequate natural theology is able to supply – an acknowledgement found with varying degrees of consensus within Judaism in the form of the eternal Torah supplying 'the precious instrument by which the world was created',[109] or Christianity's eternal Word by whom 'all things came into being' (John 1:2),[110] or Islam's speculations over the Quran's role in creation.[111] In each case, the correspondence between what the natural order and the special revelation disclose of God is sufficiently strong that the latter is deemed to be instrumental in the former.

In the light of these all-too-brief comments, we wonder whether it might be more coherent in relation to monotheistic belief to shift emphasis away from special revelation onto *sacramental amplifications* in time where extraordinary persons or events intensify divine presence – not by making present something

---

[106] This was an insight we gleaned from Alister McGrath in Section 3.

[107] See the thorough discussion of Thomas G. Weinandy, *Does God Suffer?* (Edinburgh: T. & T. Clark, 2000).

[108] On this approach, see, for example, Karl Rahner's transcendental theology outlined in *Foundations of Christian Faith: An Introduction to the Idea of Christianity*, trans. William V. Dych (New York: Crossroad, 1978).

[109] Mishnah, Aboth 3.15 (Danby); also Midrash, Genesis 1:1.

[110] John 1:2; 'We believe ... one Lord Jesus Christ, the only-begotten Son of God, begotten from his Father before all ages ... through whom all things were made', Niceno-Constantinopolitan Creed.

[111] Cf. 'Book Concealed' and 'Preserved Tablet', Quran 56:78, 85:22; also the natural theology implied, for example, in 2:164–5 or 18:109–10; see Mustafa Muhaqqiq Damad, 'The Quran and Schools of Islamic Theology and Philosophy', in *The Study Quran*, 1719–22.

previously absent, and not even by concentrating it (whatever that might mean), but by embodying it in such a way that it becomes more perceivable and serviceable. Undoubtedly, this constitutes revelation, but revelation arising within human perception, rather than flowing from fresh divine initiative. Again, a partial analogy. Consider the presence of radio waves of which most of us are oblivious without the assistance of a radio receiver capable of selecting the desired frequencies, extracting the audio signals and amplifying the same. Radio waves are no more present with the arrival of a receiver, but their presence is more apparent and beneficial for listeners when such a device is employed.

5.3 Identifying Resonances

Our final task is to draw together the two parts of this study, namely the overview of faith and belief within the Scriptures of Judaism, Christianity and Islam offered in Section 1 and the approach developed throughout the rest of the Element. Whilst we wouldn't expect to find the kind of analysis undertaken in Section 2 onwards within confessional literature, there is nonetheless considerable correspondence, which is to be expected if the largely phenomenological approach adopted throughout the bulk of this Element is well-founded. We close by highlighting a number of resonances.

First, faith as an embodied response, embracing all of life, in which intellectual assent to certain beliefs is insufficient of itself without the fruits of belief evident in the manner believers invest their time, energy and resources – whether in terms of obedience to Torah, service to Christ or submission to Allah.

Allied to this, second, the priority of faith as a trusting exploration of self-transcendence and being-in-relation to the Other affirmed in the Scriptures through the adoption of Abraham as an archetypal believer whose faith becomes manifest through a journey of leaving behind the familiar in search a new integrity, bestowed from beyond.

Third, the centrality of community as the distillers, custodians, expositors and, ultimately, arbiters of belief, constituting what we have described as a belief system – a thoroughgoing imaginary in which faith finds expression and, through the adoption of a community's beliefs and participation in its habitus, is orientated towards the transcendent. Again, as Abraham demonstrates, faith is born out of the promise of community.

Fourth, beliefs as heuristic distillations of faith's discoveries, rather than theoretical deductions of abstract thinking, where faith and belief are held within a reciprocal dialectic in which faith informs belief and belief forms faith. This is nowhere clearer than with the emergence of monotheistic belief where Abraham jettisons the synthetic deities of his upbringing in favour of one worthy of worship and capable of sustaining wholehearted allegiance.

Fifth, monotheism as the embodiment of a particular practice of faith in which, released from the distraction of idolatry in its many manifestations (including projections of the divine), believers experience a quality of sacred encounter characterized by self-transcendence and grace – one realizable through singular attention and investment of the self, giving rise to communities of worship. In this respect, the distinction between metaphysical monotheism and confessional monotheism alluded to earlier may be more apparent than real, inasmuch as the witness of Judaism, Christianity and Islam is that the only route to the former is via the latter.

Sixth, monotheistic belief delineates a way of being human, one rooted in relationality and openness to the Other. Through participating in shared disciplines and practices, values and commitments, insights and intuitions, believers become proficient in inhabiting a universe infused with the glory of God and in exploring the implications of such expansiveness for every aspect of living. Essentially, the emergence of holy law within monotheistic religions reflects an attempt to give shape and definition to this task.

These, then, are some of the areas of convergence that hopefully vindicate the approach adopted throughout this Element. The final 'final' word, though, must go to Abraham who demonstrates that all faith, especially when expressed through monotheistic belief, is at its most vital when embodied in persons, rather than enshrined in creeds.

Abbreviations

ANCL   *Ante-Nicene Christian Library*, edited by Alexander Roberts and James Donaldson, 10 vols. (Edinburgh: T. & T. Clark, 1867–85)

LCL   Loeb Classical Library, multiple vols. (London: William Heinemann & Cambridge, MA: Harvard University Press, 1912–; an asterisk * indicates a revision in the Loeb translation)

OTP   *Old Testament Pseudepigrapha*, edited by James H. Charlesworth, 2 vols. (Garden City, NY: Doubleday, 1983 and 1985)

Copyright

Acknowledgements

I am grateful to Professors Chad Meister and Paul Moser for the invitation to contribute this Element to the *Elements in Religion and Monotheism* series. It has afforded me the opportunity to crystallize thoughts that have accompanied me for much of the past twenty years, during which time I have come to the realization that to engage satisfactorily with the two foci of this study requires an interdisciplinary approach. To this end, I have attempted to draw on insights beyond my own specialism, cognisant of the dangers of 'playing away from home', yet remaining convinced of the need to do so. I trust this has been undertaken intelligently and with credibility. My conversation partners have been diverse and I readily acknowledge my indebtedness both to those identified in the text and those whose names have become disassociated in my mind with ideas espoused. I am grateful also to the staff of Cambridge University Press for their assistance in steering this project through to publication, as well as to my reviewers who have helped to clarify the argument in various places. If I harbour one hope for this Element, it is to make a contribution to faith's recognition as an essential ingredient of authentic human being and monotheism's claim to be the consummation of faith's vocation.

To Lizzie,
companion through life,
source of joy.

Cambridge Elements ☰

Religion and Monotheism

Paul K. Moser

Loyola University Chicago

Paul K. Moser is Professor of Philosophy at Loyola University Chicago. He is the author of *Understanding Religious Experience; The God Relationship; The Elusive God* (winner of national book award from the Jesuit Honor Society); *The Evidence for God; The Severity of God; Knowledge and Evidence* (all Cambridge University Press); and *Philosophy after Objectivity* (Oxford University Press); co-author of *Theory of Knowledge* (Oxford University Press); editor of *Jesus and Philosophy* (Cambridge University Press) and *The Oxford Handbook of Epistemology* (Oxford University Press); co-editor of *The Wisdom of the Christian Faith* (Cambridge University Press). He is the co-editor with Chad Meister of the book series *Cambridge Studies in Religion, Philosophy, and Society.*

Chad Meister

Bethel University

Chad Meister is Professor of Philosophy and Theology and Department Chair at Bethel College. He is the author of *Introducing Philosophy of Religion* (Routledge, 2009), *Christian Thought: A Historical Introduction*, 2nd edition (Routledge, 2017), and *Evil: A Guide for the Perplexed*, 2nd edition (Bloomsbury, 2018). He has edited or co-edited the following: *The Oxford Handbook of Religious Diversity* (Oxford University Press, 2010), *Debating Christian Theism* (Oxford University Press, 2011), with Paul Moser, *The Cambridge Companion to the Problem of Evil* (Cambridge University Press, 2017), and with Charles Taliaferro, *The History of Evil* (Routledge, 2018, in six volumes).

About the Series

This Cambridge Element series publishes original concise volumes on monotheism and its significance. Monotheism has occupied inquirers since the time of the Biblical patriarch, and it continues to attract interdisciplinary academic work today. Engaging, current, and concise, the Elements benefit teachers, research students, and advanced students in religious studies, Biblical studies, theology, philosophy of religion, and related fields.

Cambridge Elements ≡

Religion and Monotheism

Elements in the Series

CPSIA information can be obtained
at www.ICGtesting.com
Printed in the USA
LVHW080118290721
694014LV00013B/1033